Dedication

To the Caribbean, where I grew up, and its people, who understand the sacredness of cannabis.

Acknowledgments

Thank you to my agent, Eric Smith of P.S. Literary, for understanding my vision and always believing in me (and for the Scorpio jokes). I would also like to thank Rebecca Tarr Thomas, Adams Media, and Simon & Schuster for giving me the opportunity to write this book. Thank you to Melissa, Lakisha, John, and Mike for sharing your self-care rituals and cannabis knowledge with me. Thank you to Stef and my many great friends for your love, encouragement, and support through the writing process. Thank you to all the readers for joining me in changing the way we talk about and use cannabis. Finally, thank you to cannabis for being a great source of healing, inspiration, and great joy for so many years.

Contents

Praise for *Finding Your Higher Self*

"Can marijuana really improve your health and extend your life? Absolutely! And in *Finding Your Higher Self*, Sophie Saint Thomas reveals how to properly infuse cannabis and CBD into more than one hundred fun activities and soothing rituals that treat stress, heal trauma, and enhance pleasurable experiences. I discovered new and creative ways to enjoy my favorite flower and you will too!"

—Danny Danko, senior cultivation editor of *High Times*

"In *Finding Your Higher Self*, Sophie Saint Thomas effortlessly guides readers into creating affirming and spiritual experiences all inspired by the healing and downright magical effects of cannabis. Filled with research, scientific data, and only rituals of self-care a witch could write, this book helps readers find their most authentic selves while helping to remove the stigma of working with this plant. From meditation to creative rituals to new ways of interacting with cannabis, this book is an indispensable guide to self-care for mind, body, and soul. Whether you're a longtime stoner or are just now starting on your plant-medicine journey, you will find something of importance and value in these pages as you connect with your higher self."

—Gabriela Herstik, author of *Inner Witch: A Modern Guide to the Ancient Craft* and "The High Priestess" column in *High Times*

"Sophie Saint Thomas embodies what I like most in writers—infinite curiosity, earnestness (without a smidge of naivete), and strong sense of self-awareness. Plus, she's really freaking funny. Reading her work immediately makes you want to be her friend, and for good reason. Because if more people had brains as beautiful as SST's, the world would be a more interesting and titillating place. I won't hold my breath, though. She's a true gem among pebbles!"

—Zach Sokol, culture writer and managing editor of *Merry Jane*

"For too long cannabis has been viewed as a harmful substance—a flower without benefit—when all along it has illustrated the opposite to be true. Sophie does an amazing job painting this picture in *Finding Your Higher Self*, uplifting some age-old practices past their propaganda-stained stigmas, and introducing some new ways to not only find peace, but to elevate your quality of life. This is an excellent read for those looking to infuse their life with a more spiritual approach."

—Jon Cappetta, vice president of content at *High Times*

Praise for *Finding Your Higher Self*

"Cannabis has a unique ability to promote inner peace, and Sophie Saint Thomas has created the perfect primer for anyone who wants to harness the calming power of plant medicine. Whether you're canna-curious or a well-versed enthusiast, you'll find dozens of opportunities to enhance your life with cannabis in *Finding Your Higher Self*."

—Molly Peckler, founder of *Highly Devoted*

"Sophie's the cool aunt who comes into your life, teaches you about weed, and changes your whole world. No one does self-care like Sophie. *Finding Your Higher Self* will help you open your third eye, joint in hand."

—Zachary Zane, cannabis columnist at *Civilized* and contributor to *Rolling Stone*

"*Finding Your Higher Self* is exactly what I needed to satisfy my curiosity for using cannabis as a tool for self-care and discovery. Sophie Saint Thomas's style is perfect, refreshing, and enlightening. Reading this book and working through the exercises was fun and uplifting, and something I will revisit again and again."

—Vanessa Cuccia, author of *Crystal Healing & Sacred Pleasure: Awaken Your Sensual Energy Using Crystals and Healing Rituals, One Chakra at a Time*

"Sophie Saint Thomas is single-handedly helping bring conscious cannabis users out of the closet and into the mainstream with her depth of knowledge; disarming wit; and generous, ethics-driven spirit. This book offers a safe space, for both the weed-curious and lifelong weed lovers, to explore one of nature's greatest healers and helpers through the lens of self-care. Just as it should be."

—Jerico Mandybur, author, spiritual self-care coach, and cannabis advocate

"This book is fantastic, especially for the growing number of people who are curious about using cannabis as a tool for supporting and nurturing themselves. Sophie Saint Thomas is a thoughtful, inventive writer with excellent practical tips for incorporating cannabis into your self-care regimen on all levels: physical, emotional, and even spiritual. A highly accessible resource designed to meet readers where they are."

—Ashley Manta, CannaSexual founder

Adams Media

New York Amsterdam/Antwerp London Toronto Sydney/Melbourne New Delhi

Adams Media
An Imprint of Simon & Schuster, LLC
100 Technology Center Drive
Stoughton, MA 02072

This Adams Media trade paperback edition December 2025

ADAMS MEDIA and colophon are registered trademarks of Simon & Schuster, LLC.

Simon & Schuster strongly believes in freedom of expression and stands against censorship in all its forms. For more information, visit BooksBelong.com.

For information about special discounts for bulk purchases, please contact Simon & Schuster Special Sales at 1-866-506-1949 or business@simonandschuster.com.

The Simon & Schuster Speakers Bureau can bring authors to your live event. For more information or to book an event, contact the Simon & Schuster Speakers Bureau at 1-866-248-3049 or visit our website at www.simonspeakers.com.

Interior design by Colleen Cunningham and Priscilla Yuen
Hand lettering by Priscilla Yuen

Manufactured in the United States of America

1 2025

ISBN 978-1-5072-2626-1
ISBN 978-1-5072-1141-0 (ebook)

Introduction

Relax your spirit with a cannabis-based meditation.
Enhance your mind with a CBD smoothie.
Check in with your body by consuming edibles.

For centuries cannabis, and the oils and tinctures derived from its buds and flowers, has been used to help manage insomnia, relieve anxiety, sharpen focus, heighten creative thinking, and much more. And today the powers of this little plant have been harnessed to help you care for and embrace the three corners of your existence—your mind, body, and soul—through the act of self-care.

Self-care is the practice of slowing down and taking steps to put yourself first. It's allowing yourself to prioritize your well-being. Self-care helps you integrate love, both for yourself and for others, into your life. It gives you what you need to live the best, most full life you can imagine. In the busyness of today it's easy to forget the importance of pausing to ensure all of your needs are met. It may feel like there's never enough time. However, if you don't take time to tend to yourself, you risk burning out. That's where cannabis comes in.

Whether you are familiar with cannabis or ready to experiment, *Finding Your Higher Self* will guide you through more than one hundred cannabis-enhanced self-care rituals that act as a salve for your mind, body, and spirit. Here you'll learn to create your own cannabis topical and how to apply it to sore and stiff muscles after a good stretch. You'll have cannabis by your side to help you work through difficult emotions and let go of shame. You'll expand your mind while reigniting your creativity. You'll practice mindfulness and learn how to be fully present in your here and now.

And if you're unsure about the specifics—which strain of cannabis is right for you, the difference between THC and CBD, or whether you should try edibles or a joint—you'll find all those questions and more answered here as well. Then all you have to do is sit back, take a deep breath, and infuse your mind, body, and spirit with the soothing powers of this herb.

How to Use This Book

Before you begin or expand your practice of cannabis-influenced self-care, you need to learn some basics in order to tailor your self-care activities to your own personalized needs. So let's take a closer look at what self-care is, the different types and benefits of cannabis, and how using cannabis for self-care can help you elevate your mind, body, and spirit in ways you may not even have considered.

What Is Self-Care?

As you know, self-care is the act of putting yourself first. While self-care can be luxurious, it is not petty. It is tending to yourself as you would a loved one so you can thrive professionally and personally. Breaks aren't lazy; they are necessary to sustain your health, relationships, and ambition. Taking the time to stretch or exercise keeps your body strong. Meditation breaks ease worries and keep your mind sharp. Creating art feeds your soul and keeps your spirits high as you make the most of this life. These are just a few of the self-care activities, amplified by cannabis, that we'll discuss in this book. Let's take a look at the different types of self-care and how cannabis can help you connect with and nurture the whole you.

BODY

In today's fast-paced world it's easy to get stuck in your head and feel disconnected from your body. You may not even realize how physically out of touch you are until you make the decision to take a moment for yourself. To get out of your mind and inhabit your body. To be present in the vessel that you've been given. How? By practicing self-care.

Cannabis helps you do this by keeping you present, in your body, and in a good mood. The plant can be applied topically to alleviate pain or to keep you focused and mindful of the healing power of a bath. Use the body-based self-care rituals in Part 1—such as body scan meditation, stretching, or exploring your erogenous zones—to enhance your connection to your physical self. You'll also find information here on how to make topicals and tinctures to keep your body healthy, relaxed, and operating at its full function.

MIND

Artists and visionaries are right about cannabis's mind-expanding properties. Cannabis causes the prefrontal cortex to release a hormone called dopamine, which can help you tap into your creative side. In Part 2 you'll experience how creative self-expression lowers stress and boosts self-confidence, leaving you feeling at the top of your game. You'll also find self-care activities ranging from journaling to learning a new instrument to starting a podcast with friends that are made possible by the intense focus that cannabis can bring. These rituals will help you take care of tasks and chores and enjoy yourself while you do so. And if you need help turning off your mind and focusing inward, you'll also learn guided meditations and breath work in this section that will help you quiet your mind and sink into total relaxation.

SPIRIT

Your spirit is you in your most sincere form, which makes feeding your spirit with self-care activities that make you joyful so incredibly important. Cannabis helps provide a foundation for your spiritual self-care practice by aiding in sleep, reducing anxiety, and encouraging self-love. A 2013 study published in the journal *European Neuropsychopharmacology* suggests that cannabis reduces our negative bias in emotional processing, which can help us consider life from a more positive perspective. This glass-half-full attitude can improve your relationships with loved ones. You can also use the plant to enhance the soul-nurturing benefits of spending time bathing in the warm sun or ethereal starlight and connecting with those who love you for exactly who you are.

Now that you know how cannabis can nurture your mind, body, and spirit through intentional acts of self-care, it's time to take a deeper look at how cannabis affects your body and how to choose the type of cannabis that will work best for the self-care ritual you have planned.

Making Cannabis Work for You

Whether you've been using cannabis for some time or are looking to learn more, it's important to understand how cannabis interacts with your body and why. Your body has a natural biological system called the endocannabinoid system, which it uses to process cannabinoids, chemical compounds that are found in cannabis, such as THC (tetrahydrocannabinol) and CBD (cannabidiol). When you consume cannabis, these compounds bind to the cannabinoid receptors in the central nervous system and peripheral nervous system, which then cause the effects of cannabis to be felt throughout the body.

THC AND CBD

There are at least 104 cannabinoids that can be processed by your endocannabinoid system, but THC and CBD, which share the same molecular structure, are the best known. THC is psychoactive and provides the high that marijuana is famous for. CBD is non-psychoactive but has become in demand as an anti-anxiety remedy. Both THC and CBD can be sold as isolates, which is an extract of the cannabinoid in pure form, but while isolates have their place, many cannabis users and researchers believe THC and CBD work best when consumed in tandem.

Please note that even if cannabis plants from different regions have the same name, the strains may differ in THC and CBD levels depending on where they are grown. Each body, mind, and spirit also reacts differently to these cannabinoids, so make note of what works for you. Your body knows best. If you find a product that makes you feel good, stick with it.

Let's take a closer look at these two cannabinoids.

Tetrahydrocannabinol (THC)

THC is the cannabinoid that provides the effects you're probably used to associating with cannabis. Many people find its mellow high the perfect end to a day, and others swear by its social anxiety–relieving mood boost. It's also responsible for the mind-expanding properties of cannabis that open you creatively. When you're ready to draw or attend a concert, use cannabis with THC. When it's dosed correctly for you, THC will infuse your self-care activities with a feeling of euphoria, heightened senses, and mental stimulation.

***Effects*:** Euphoria, elation, laughter, focus, change in time perception, energy, dry mouth, anxiety, paranoia, hunger, red eyes.

***Strains with High Levels*:** Chemdawg, Girl Scout Cookies, Superglue, Gorilla Glue, Godfather OG, Ghost Train Haze, Purple Chem, White Fire OG.

Cannabidiol (CBD)

CBD may be non-psychoactive, but that doesn't mean it's non-beneficial. CBD alone is used to treat inflammation, pain, anxiety, and more. And if you don't care for the buzz of THC, you may find relief from sore knees through a CBD topical or enjoy a CBD tincture as a sleep aid. It's also demonstrative of the many ways the cannabis plants can aid in self-care through promoting relaxation, anti-inflammation properties, and anxiety reduction.

***Effects*:** Anti-anxiety, calm, relaxation, drowsiness, pain relief, anti-inflammatory.

***Strains with High Levels*:** Cannatonic, Cali Cure, Ringo's Gift, Remedy, AC/DC, CBD Shark, Desert Ruby.

DIFFERENT TYPES EXPLAINED

Cannabis is typically broken down into three types: indicas, sativas, and hybrids. Various strains, such as Northern Lights (indica) and Sour Diesel (sativa), fit into each of these categories. A hybrid is a blend of sativa and indica, with one or the other dominant. Let's take a look at how each of these unique cannabis types will help you on your self-care journey.

Indica

Indica invokes the feeling of bodily highs and love baths, tea and relaxation, and chilled-out nights on the couch. Use an indica when you're in need of full-body stress relief and wouldn't mind cuddling up to watch a movie.

Appearance: Indicas are short, round plants, with wide leaves and a short flowering cycle. They are better suited for cold climates and short seasons.

Associated Properties: Indicas are associated with relaxation and body highs. They are often used for anxiety, sleep, and pain relief.

Strain Examples: Northern Lights, Granddaddy Purple, Kush, Blueberry, Blue Cheese, Death Star, God's Gift, Do-Si-Dos.

Sativa

Sativas stimulate creative tendencies and energetic flows and pack a punch of positivity to help you in your daytime adventures and creative endeavors. Use a sativa strain when you want to feel calm yet engaged and flutter among friends like a social butterfly. Sativas are a wonderful addition to outdoor music or a majestic hike, or to help with inspiration while crafting or cleaning.

***Appearance*:** Sativas are tall, thin plants with skinny leaves and a long flowering cycle. They are better suited for warm climates and long seasons.

***Associated Properties*:** Sativas are associated with mental invigoration and creative cerebral effects. They are often used for focus and fighting fatigue.

***Strain Examples*:** Sour Diesel, Durban Poison, Maui Wowie, Grapefruit, Green Crack, Purple Haze, Casey Jones.

Hybrid

Hybrids contain the magic of both sativa and indica and are an all-around choice for any self-care ritual. If you're planning to attend a party and want cannabis that will keep you social yet also help you take a big breath of calm, try a sativa-dominant hybrid. If you're unwinding and want an after-dinner smoke to encourage relaxation but not put you straight to sleep, try an indica-dominant hybrid.

***Appearance*:** A hybrid cannabis plant is a genetic mixture of indica and sativa. They take on properties from both.

***Associated Properties*:** Hybrid effects vary greatly from strain to strain. Some are indica-dominant, some sativa-dominant; others are the best of both worlds.

***Strain Examples*:** Pineapple Express, Cheese, Gelato, Sour Kush, Headband, Blue Dream, Girl Scout Cookies, Gorilla Glue.

Exceptions to the Rule

While people typically categorize cannabis as indica, sativa, or hybrid—and these are the types of cannabis you'll see discussed throughout the book—it's important to note that, as researchers learn more about the cannabis plant, the lines between the strains become a little blurry. This is why, when you can, it's important to look at the cannabinoid profile of each strain to truly understand a plant's properties. For instance, an indica-dominant hybrid called Ace of Spades may have a 15% THC level and 0.003% CBD level, while the sativa-dominant hybrid called AC/DC may have a 0.8% THC level and a 19% CBD level. You may assume that the indica-dominant hybrid would have more relaxing CBD, but that's not always the case. When possible look for such information through dispensaries and doctors to find cannabis that is tailor-made to your needs.

VARIOUS INTAKE OPTIONS AND THEIR EFFECTS

Just as there are different types of cannabis, there are different ways to consume them, and each intake method will affect your experience. Your delivery method may change with each self-care act, so begin to familiarize yourself with the various options below.

INHALED OPTIONS

Inhalation methods, such as the options discussed in this section, all work instantly and are great if you are want to feel the effects of the cannabis immediately. When inhaled, cannabis smoke enters your lungs, where the cannabinoids are absorbed into the bloodstream. However, while smoking offers near instantaneous effects, those effects also fade faster than with other intake methods.

Joint

What Is It? A joint is a cannabis cigarette. They are often hand-rolled, but as legalization spreads, prerolled joints are increasingly available. Joints are rolled with whole flower (ground cannabis buds).

Pros: Joints are great for passing around at a party or with friends. Once rolled, they are easy to hold and use.

Cons: Using the whole flower gives a joint that distinct cannabis smell, which can attract unwanted attention at times.

Spliff

What Is It? A spliff is traditionally a joint that contains cannabis mixed with tobacco. However, you can make spliffs using other herbs as add-ins.

Pros: Mixing cannabis with lavender, damiana, and/or mugwort offers an array of highs and experiences. If smoking one joint is too intense, blends allow you to comfortably puff on an entire joint without getting too high.

Cons: Smoking tobacco comes with all the health risks of cigarettes, such as cancer and heart problems.

Blunt

What Is It? Blunts are cannabis cigarettes rolled using cigar paper (tobacco leaf).

Pros: Cigar paper is readily available.

Cons: Smoking tobacco comes with all the health risks of cigarettes, such as cancer and heart problems.

Pipe

What Is It? Pipes, which are often made of glass, contain a bowl for ground flower, a mouthpiece, and a carb, which is a hole that clears the chamber as you smoke.

Pros: Pipes are extremely easy to use and pack.

Cons: Pipes require cleaning and upkeep.

Bong

What Is It? A bong is a water pipe, meaning the cannabis smoke is cooled and filtered through water.

Pros: The water in a bong can provide a smoother draw than pipes that do not use water filtration. Compared to pipes, some bongs hold much more cannabis smoke, giving you a greater high.

Cons: While bongs are beautiful and look great on display, they are not the most discreet inhalation option. And like pipes, they require cleaning and upkeep.

Bubbler

What Is It? A bubbler is a water pipe like a bong; however, it is smaller and resembles more traditional pipes.

Pros: Bubblers, like bongs, also use water to filter smoke and give a smoother hit. But since bubblers are smaller than bongs, they are easier to store.

Cons: Bubblers are often more difficult to clean than pipes.

OTHER INTAKE OPTIONS

While there are many benefits of inhaling your cannabis, that method may not work for you all the time. For example, if you are in a situation in which you must be cautious about the smell, a vaporizer is less intense but still instant. Edibles are extremely discreet; however, they take a long time to kick in and likewise last for quite a while. Here you'll find additional options that, depending on your needs, may work better for your self-care practice.

Dabs

What Is It? Dabs are concentrated cannabis created using butane or carbon dioxide to form a sticky, wax-like substance that is high in THC. These potent, waxy substances are also called wax or shatter. Dabs are heated at high temperature often using a blowtorch and then inhaled through a rig, or a water pipe crafted specifically for dabs.

Effects: The high of dabs is instantaneous and provides a more powerful hit than other inhalation methods.

***Pros*:** Many medicinal users appreciate the swiftness and power of this method. Extracts can also be cleaner on the lungs than traditional cannabis smoke.

***Cons*:** The extraction process is dangerous and should be left to the experts. The most common method to heat concentrates is a blowtorch, which carries safety concerns. As concentrates are usually 50%–90% THC, the high may be too intense for some.

Vaporizer

What Is It? Vaporizers, or vapes, are devices that use heat to turn cannabis flower or cartridges into vapor rather than smoke.

***Effects*:** Like inhalation, the effects of vaping cannabis are pretty instant; however, vapes tend to be slightly less intense than smoking. The vapor is healthier for your lungs, and users report a slightly less intense high from cannabis oil in vape cartridges than from smoking whole flower.

***Pros*:** Vapor is easier on the lungs than smoke. Most vaporizers today are portable and easy to use on the go.

***Cons*:** While many prefer the cleaner hit of a vaporizer, others prefer the headiness of smoke inhalation.

Tincture

What Is It? Tinctures are alcohol- or oil-based cannabis extracts.

***Effects*:** Tinctures can be placed sublingually (under the tongue) or added to beverages. Sublingual effects kick in after 15 minutes, but it will take up to an hour and a half for you to feel the full effect.

***Pros*:** Tinctures are a low-calorie option that turn any beverage into a cannabis cocktail.

***Cons*:** Tinctures may not be for those who avoid alcohol; however, other fat solubles such as vinegar or glycerol may be used instead of alcohol.

Edibles

What Is It? An edible is any food made with cannabis.

***Effects*:** Edibles take up to an hour and a half to provide full effects, and last for several hours. The body high is greater than with other intake methods.

***Pros*:** You can discreetly take edibles with you on the go. Or, as they take a while to start working but last for many hours, edibles are great to eat before an outing.

***Cons*:** Enjoying edibles requires responsible dosing. Consuming too much can make for an unpleasant experience. (See info on dosing in the following section.)

Topicals

What Is It? Topicals are body creams or oils that are non-psychoactive when applied to the skin because they do not enter the bloodstream.

***Effects*:** Topicals reduce inflammation, pain, soreness, and stiffness.

***Pros*:** Topicals and their pain-relieving properties demonstrate the many medical benefits of the cannabis plant.

Cons: Because cannabis has become quite trendy, the beauty market is rushing to capitalize by adding CBD to skin care products. Due to lack of regulation it's often difficult to know where such cannabis comes from; finding a trustworthy supplier can be a challenge. Cannabis skin care products are also quite pricy, which is why you're going to learn how to make your own.

BASIC DOSING ADVICE

Like any substance, it's hard to enjoy cannabis if you accidentally take too much, so you'll want to do your best to prevent that from happening. Here you'll learn the basics so you can know what is a good starting dose for you.

When inhaling cannabis, start by taking one or two hits, and see how you feel. As the experience kicks in quickly, you will be able to gauge what's right for you right away. Remember that, should you overconsume, the effects of inhalation fade as fast as they come. Keep in mind that some methods of inhalation, such as dabs or a bong, give more intense highs. A vaporizer is also easy to gauge and generally provides a lighter high. For tinctures, start with two to three drops under your tongue, adding more after an hour if needed.

Edibles are the trickiest method of intake to figure out dosing for because the effects take up to an hour and a half to be felt and last for several hours, so you don't want to overconsume. Thankfully, most edibles are well labeled these days. In some states where cannabis is legal the suggested starting dose is 10 mg. For someone with a low tolerance, though, that can still be a lot, so start with 5 mg and work your way up as needed. Remember, it's easier to consume more than to undo a high (although water, food, and CBD can help with that). So whichever way you choose to intake your cannabis, you should start with a small dose, add as needed, and keep a journal of your experience as your tolerance levels will probably change over time.

CREATE YOUR OWN CANNABIS OIL

Keeping a supply of cannabis oil at the ready will ensure that you can practice self-care whenever you have the chance. Your time is valuable—and likely often limited—which is why having cannabis oil on hand is so important for your self-care practice. These instructions are given to you here, in this section of the book, so you can have this oil available whenever you need it. After all, once you have cannabis oil, making your own edibles is as simple as using your infused magical-ingredient oil instead of whatever oil is called for in a recipe. Creating topicals to ease body pains becomes so much easier when you have cannabis oil on hand to drop into a lotion or body oil. Or you can place a few drops of cannabis oil under your tongue like a tincture, and get into a meditative state of calm. Cannabis oil is dosed like tinctures; start with a few drops, see how you feel, and work your way up to an entire vial.

Note that, while we associate edibles with sweets, you can also use this oil to transform savory dishes.

Use the strain of cannabis that's best for your body and budget, then switch out the regular oil in any recipe for this cannabis oil to make an edible.

YOU WILL NEED

- 1 cup of ground cannabis flower, roughly 8 grams (adjust as desired for potency)
- A grinder or mortar and pestle
- A strainer or cheesecloth
- 1 cup of oil (Note that you can create cannabis oil with any oil, but the two most commonly used are coconut and olive.)
- A dash of water to help prevent burning
- A slow cooker, double boiler, or saucepan

HOW TO

1. Grind your cannabis using a grinder created for cannabis, or a mortar and pestle. If using a grinder, be sure to grind over the strainer or cheesecloth to catch any chunks of herb. If using a mortar and pestle, pour through the strainer or cheesecloth once the cannabis has been ground. Grind the cannabis to the consistency you would use to make a joint (a fine crumble); it should not be a powder fine enough to slip through the cheesecloth or strainer.
2. Combine the oil and cannabis in a medium-sized bowl and add a splash or two of water, just enough to prevent burning.

3. Now start the process of decarboxylation, which uses heat to activate the THC. (This process happens on its own through smoking or baking, but in order for the cannabis to have a psychoactive effect when used in oils and other edibles, decarboxylation must be induced. In any case, you can't just eat a cannabis bud and get high.) If you're using a **slow cooker**, pour in the mixture, then set the slow cooker on low for at least 5 hours, but ideally 8 hours or more. Stir periodically. If you're using a **double boiler**, add mixture then cook for at least 6 hours (preferably 8 hours), stirring frequently, roughly a few times an hour. If you're using a **saucepan**, add your mixture and cook on low for at least 3 hours, frequently stirring as this method is most susceptible to burning. There is not a universal recipe for creating cannabis oil, so keep your eye on the stove. If the substance looks like burning is a risk, stir and add a little more water.
4. Place cheesecloth (or your strainer) over a pot and pour the cooked oil mixture through to filter out the cannabis residue. Once cooled, package in a cool, dark place, such as an opaque bottle, and store your oil in the fridge for up to two months, or the freezer for up to three months. You can add your cannabis oil to edible recipes or skin-soothing topicals, or use it as part of a self-care ritual (by anointing a candle, for example).

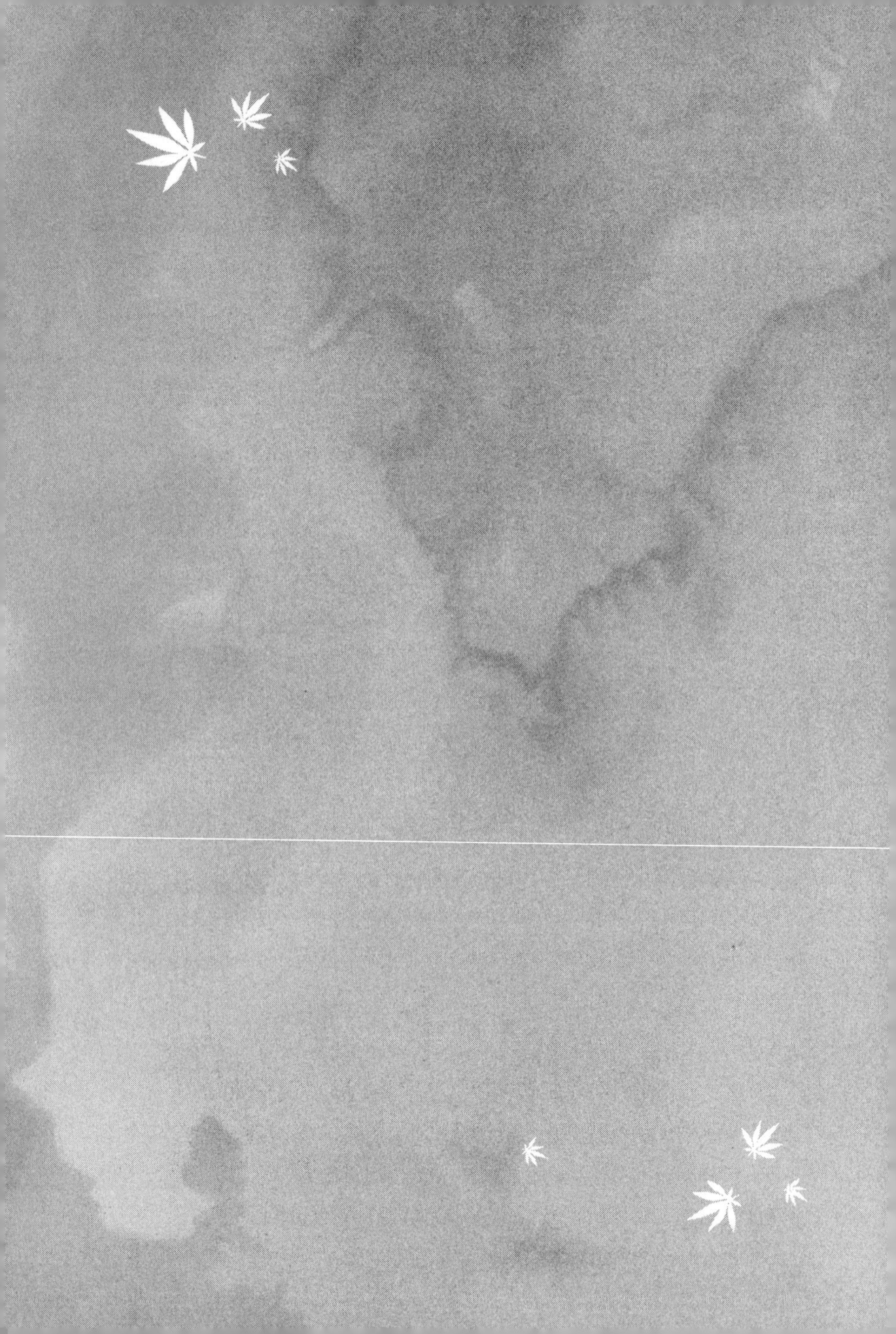

PART 1

Body

AT LEAST 30 MINUTES

Draw a Cannabis Bath

Benefits: A bath cleans more than the dirt your body collects throughout the day. It also calms and cleanses your mind. Warm baths have been shown to treat muscle and joint pain, and soaking in steamy waters strengthens your immune system.

How does cannabis help? As a non-psychoactive topical such as a bath bomb, cannabis has inflammation-soothing and pain-relieving properties that heal the body. In psychoactive forms, cannabis helps to induce calm and relieve stress to help you bathe in relaxation.

HOW TO

1. Arrange your bathroom to create a tranquil space. Light candles to set the mood and keep a soft towel and fluffy robe nearby. Put on calming music.
2. Grab your ingestible cannabis and a topical cannabis bath bomb or bath salts. Place a folded towel next to the bath, so you have a safe space to place your medicine without water affecting it.
3. Turn on the hot water and find a temperature of your liking. As the water fills the tub, rather than waiting impatiently sit on the edge of the tub and take some tokes of cannabis. As the water rises, so will your state of mind. Watch the water swirl around and fill the tub. Contemplate how many religions and cultures around the world use the element of water for rituals.

4. When you're ready, step into the bathtub. Use your heightened state of awareness to pay attention to how the water feels gently flowing over your body as it fills the tub. Cannabis enhances the senses, so notice how the warm water feels engulfing your body.
5. If you have a cannabis bath bomb or bath salts, plop them into the flowing water. Know that the plant is working its anti-inflammatory properties on your body and taking care of you using its own pain-relieving and healing properties. Watch the science of a bath bomb or salts changing forms to become part of the water.
6. Sit back, relax, and enjoy the bath while continuing to partake in cannabis as desired. Take this time to appreciate your surroundings, the sound of tranquil music, the flickering of candles dancing around the room. You're bathing in serenity. You're soaking in a magical cauldron of calm.
7. When you're ready, get out and notice how your body and mind have left your worries behind and are ready for more relaxation.

20 MINUTES

Brew a Cup of Tea

Benefits: Both green and chamomile tea contain antioxidant properties, and they're also able to help get you into the zone or decompress. It can feel counterintuitive to step away from a busy day but taking 20 minutes for self-care will make you more productive in the long run.

How does cannabis help? If you use indica cannabis oil you'll enhance this ritual with an extra dose of calm. If you need an energy boost, use sativa cannabis oil to stimulate your mind and creativity. Studies show that cannabis is an antioxidant. It not only raises your mind to a higher state but is also beneficial for your overall physical health.

HOW TO

1. The act of brewing, steeping, and unwinding with a cup of tea is a ritual used across centuries and countries. You can use this ancient art to relax or for an energy boost, depending on what type of self-care your body needs in the moment. So first, identify what your body needs right now. Is it motivation? Choose caffeinated green tea to give you an energy boost. Do you need something to help you relax or to soothe anxiety? Turn to relaxing chamomile when it's time to unwind. Once you've selected your tea, boil water and make a cup as you usually would.
2. For this self-care ritual you'll want to use a cannabis tincture (see Create a Cannabis Tincture in Part 2). You can make tea

out of cannabis, but it's rather complicated and doesn't always come out as potent as you'd like since THC is not water soluble. So take your tincture and drop as much cannabis as you feel you need into your tea. If you're busy and using green tea, perhaps a few drops is all that's needed. If it's the end of the day and you're ready to check out, go for an entire vial. While sometimes all you want is a few drops, when dosing your tincture the standard protocol is to begin with 1 ml, and see how that affects you. Then try more as needed.

3. Next, find somewhere you can sit alone with your cup of tea. Ideally, tea should be enjoyed without multitasking, mindfully taking each sip. Leave your phone and computer behind. Savor each sip. Treat enjoying your cup of tea as a sacred ritual.
4. When you finish, go back to your scheduled programming, and enjoy the rest of your day or night from a heightened and relaxed perspective.

Get Into Child's Pose

Benefits: Child's Pose takes you back to the serenity of the womb. This yoga pose compresses the chest and causes you to breathe deeply, which slows down your heart rate and causes your body to automatically relax. Child's Pose also helps with back and neck pain, and stretches the shoulders, hips, and ankles.

How does cannabis help? Cannabis helps you become more mindful of your body and have a richer and deeper experience in this pose. Cannabis lowers inhibitions, which can allow you to let go into a childlike place of rest.

HOW TO

1. Find a quiet place where you can set up your yoga mat and sit cross-legged with your cannabis without interruption. The creative properties of cannabis turn any place you can fit a yoga mat into your personal yoga studio.
2. Take a moment to do some deep breathing. Use your cannabis to guide your breath. Take a hit of your medicine and inhale slowly, letting the smoke or vapor fill your lungs. Exhale slowly as you blow out the smoke. Use this breathing pattern for several rounds until the body exudes a sense of calm.
3. When you're ready, enter Child's Pose by getting on your hands and knees. Then spread your knees wide apart and bring your feet together. Sink back, allowing your butt to touch your feet.

4. As your bottom sinks backward, stretch your hands forward, reaching as far as you can. Let your head fall in between your arms and place your forehead gently on the ground.
5. Feel the stretch and lengthening in your arms, shoulders, neck, and back. Remember to continue conscious breathing.
6. Get silly. It's called Child's Pose for a reason. No one is judging you. Let the cannabis help you wiggle around and feel goofy as you stretch your hips, torso, neck, shoulders, and arms, paying extra attention to those spots that need a little extra love.
7. When you're ready, gently curl up until you're seated. Notice the state of relaxation you entered. Spend a few moments sitting on your mat before returning to standing. Highlight that lightened mind with another hit of cannabis to bookend the experience.

20 MINUTES

Mindfully Prepare, Roll, and Smoke a Joint

***Benefits*:** Once you're able to roll your own joint, you no longer rely on others passing around theirs. Bowls, bongs, vapes, and edibles are lovely, but there's something about a classic joint that can enhance your self-care. Rolling a joint takes practice and, when approached with mindfulness, can be a meditative activity you can teach to others.

How does cannabis help? Rolling a joint takes concentration, mindfulness, and practice, which makes this a perfect self-care ritual. Cannabis, in particular sativa strains, can help you focus and be present to learn the skills needed to perfect the art of joint rolling.

HOW TO

1. Find somewhere with a flat surface such as a table (consider investing in a rolling tray), and gather your cannabis, a grinder, rolling papers, and a smoking device (with which to consume cannabis before rolling).
2. Grind your cannabis into an even, fluffy consistency. Discard any stems or seeds.
3. Using your smoking device of choice, inhale some cannabis before rolling to get into the zone.
4. Create your filter (also known as a crutch) by cutting a small (roughly 2-inch by 1-inch) piece of cardboard from your pack

of papers. You can also use an index or business card, or buy premade filters, if you prefer. Then either generate accordion-like bends in the paper (make an M shape) and roll it up to form the filter, or simply roll the paper to make the tube-shaped filter.

5. Place the filter at the end of your rolling paper, then scatter your ground cannabis (about a half a gram works well) into the paper.
6. Joint papers come with one end that contains glue. Fold the non-glue side in. Using your mouth, lightly lick the glue side to activate the adhesive.
7. With the non-glue side tucked first, roll the paper around the ground cannabis, using your fingers to massage it into a cone-like shape. When you're ready, tighten and create the joint by wrapping the moistened glue side over to secure the paper.
8. Celebrate learning how to roll a joint by smoking the one you just created.

10 MINUTES

Do Cat/Cow Pose

Benefits: By itself, the yoga pose known as Cat/Cow benefits the gastrointestinal (GI) tract, stimulates the adrenal gland, and helps improve posture. It also opens the chest where you likely carry tension, perhaps related to past hurt or trauma. This pose helps bring in fresh energy and release stagnant old stress.

How does cannabis help? Cannabis helps regulate the digestive system and is used medicinally to encourage healthy GI function and treat GI conditions such as inflammatory bowel disease (especially Crohn's disease), irritable bowel syndrome, and nausea. Combining Cat/Cow with cannabis allows you to physically release toxins and expand your heart chakra through movement and breath.

HOW TO

1. Go to a quiet, comfortable spot where you can unroll your yoga mat with plenty of room. If you like, put on some ambient music.
2. Take a moment to sit and center yourself. Inhale a few puffs of cannabis. Bring yourself into the present, and let go of thoughts you don't need. Inhale, take another puff, and imagine yourself fully in your body, your weight supported by the floor beneath your yoga mat. Let bothersome thoughts float away like leaves in the wind. Visualize grounding roots coming out of you and all the way through the layers of the Earth, connecting you to our planet's core.

3. Position yourself for the Cat/Cow Pose sequence. Get on your hands and knees, with your knees directly under your hips, and your wrists directly under your shoulders. Keep your knees hip-width apart.
4. Begin with Cow Pose: Let your stomach drop toward the ground as you inhale. Point your head and neck up toward the sky. Imagine a happy cow in a pasture as you open your shoulders. Feel the stretch from your neck down to your tailbone.
5. Move to Cat Pose: Suck your belly upward with an exhale. Imagine a majestic cat as you stretch out your spine.
6. Flow back and forth between the two poses for at least 5 minutes. Feel secure in the knowledge that you're taking care of your body and setting aside a sacred space for your self-care. With the benefit of a higher state of mind, revel in such knowledge as you continue the poses.

15–30 MINUTES

Add Herbs to Your Spliff

Benefits: A spliff traditionally means tobacco rolled with cannabis, but you can make substitutions by adding an herbal element to your self-care. The benefits here vary depending on which herb you choose: Lavender is calming, damiana and dried rose petals are aphrodisiacs, and mugwort is a sleep aid.

How does cannabis help? Cannabis aids in relaxation, helps heighten arousal, and is a sleep aid. Combining it with like-minded herbs enhances those particular qualities and allows you to vary your self-care based on what your body needs in the moment.

HOW TO

1. Obtain the herb you wish to roll a spliff with, then sit somewhere quiet and comfy with your cannabis, herbal remedy of choice, grinder, rolling papers, and a lighter.
2. Hold your cannabis buds to your nose and deeply inhale, noticing what flavors and scents you pick up on. Is it citrusy and energizing? Woody and calming?
3. Do the same with your second herb. How does its scent make you feel? Joyful? Serene? Activated?
4. Hold your cannabis buds and the second herb under your nose together. How do they work in conjunction? What memories do they invoke? What do they inspire?
5. Grind your cannabis and second herb into nice, loose, fluffy materials ready to roll. Observe the colors and textures of

your homemade herbal mixture. Then blend the two together and roll a spliff (see Mindfully Prepare, Roll, and Smoke a Joint in this part).

6. When you smoke your spliff, make sure to write down how this new herb affected you for future knowledge. As you smoke your spliff pay attention to how it affects your body. Feel its effects taking over your core, fingers, and toes, and listen to your body thank you for providing the personalized self-care ritual that it craved.

Plant and Tend an Outdoor Cannabis Garden

Benefits: Gardening is good exercise and reduces stress, enhances brain health, and may lessen dementia risk and symptoms. You'll also feel a heightened connection with the plant, as well as the joy of smoking your own buds for years to come.

How does cannabis help? Gardening in an elevated state of mind enhances the experience by heightening all five of your body's senses. Cannabis will help you practice self-care by allowing you to be present in the moment, and appreciative of the sunshine on your back and the dirt on your hands.

HOW TO

1. Make sure your climate works for cannabis. Temperatures need to be between 55°F and 86°F, or else the plants may die.
2. Choose feminized autoflowering seeds to make the growing process much more manageable. Pick a strain that you adore.
3. Plant your seeds in direct sunlight in good sturdy pots. Add fertilizer created especially for cannabis plants or simply use standard fertilizer. Water plants until the soil is soaked and there's some reservoir water at the top. Repeat once the soil becomes dry.
4. Enjoy your buds! Plants tend to flower twice a year, so it's good to plant one crop in early spring and another in summer. Autoflowering seeds will produce buds as soon as they hit maturity.

AT LEAST 20 MINUTES

Take a Shower with Your Partner

Benefits: Through the calming power of warm water, steam, and in this case, touch, showers rinse dirt and debris from your body while also rinsing away stress. The act of cleaning one another, bonding naked under the fall of water, and washing one another's hair enhances intimacy in relationships.

How does cannabis help? Cannabis heightens your sense of touch and the emotional intimacy you share with your partner. Additionally, cannabis bath and body products offer anti-inflammatory properties to soothe the body.

HOW TO

1. If you've ever heard of having a shower beer, consider a shower joint shared with your partner an elegant upgrade. After a romantic time together, whether it was sex or a dinner date, unwind into relaxation by sharing a shower. Turn on the water and adjust the temperature as desired. For some couples, this means compromise, which cannabis can help with.
2. Grab a joint, your vape, or a spliff—whatever you enjoy best. Then, as the steam fills the room, if you're still clothed, slowly undress one another.
3. Step into the shower. Light the joint and alternate taking turns under the warm water and smoking the joint.
4. Set the joint down, and take turns washing one another. Wash your partner's hair. As you do so, mindfully appreciate your partner's body and all the comforting emotions it provides.

For extra flower power, try CBD or cannabis bath and body products if you have them.

5. After you're all done washing, finish the joint and spend a few minutes just enjoying the hot water and the high. How does the water feel falling down on you? How soothing did a scalp massage feel when your partner washed your hair?
6. Get out of the shower, but don't stop mindfully caring for one another with an elevated mind-set. Take turns toweling off each other. Apply cannabis body lotion to moisturize. Enjoy the rest of your evening carrying the calm from the lovers' shower and cannabis with you.

Take a Walk

***Benefits*:** Walking keeps your heart and lungs healthy, builds stronger bones and muscles, and reduces the risk of heart disease and stroke. Walking outdoors is especially stress-relieving.

How does cannabis help? Cannabis, especially sativas, helps you get out of your head and into your surroundings due to the plant's ability to encourage activity.

HOW TO

1. Take your cannabis on your walk or have an edible before.
2. Go somewhere serene such as your favorite park, hiking trail, nature walk, or a city block that makes you smile.
3. Along the way, reevaluate what may be familiar surroundings. Can you find a spiderweb to admire? How beautiful is the light shining through the tree leaves? Do you notice any new flowers? Allow the cannabis to lower your inhibitions and put you in a childlike state of wonder.
4. Notice how your body feels. Is there a mood boost from the endorphins from the cardio of walking? Can you feel the wind against your face? Are you breaking a light sweat? Let the cannabis take you into your body and allow yourself to fully feel all the wonderful effects of taking a stroll.

Care for Your Cannabis Tools

***Benefits*:** Over time, resin will build up in your smoking devices, which, in addition to being an eyesore, makes it more challenging to get a clean, smooth inhale. Regularly clean your cannabis tools for aesthetic and health reasons. They'll last longer and are better on the lungs.

How does cannabis help? Cleaning your smoking supplies with an elevated mind can become a mindfulness practice. The plant also helps you focus due to the release of dopamine, a chemical in the brain related to mood and motivation.

HOW TO

1. Enjoy a toke before you clean. This will aid in mindfulness and connect you with cannabis and your smoking method of choice.
2. To begin, first put on latex or kitchen gloves. Then use a small metal tool (you can buy cleaning supplies at your local head shop, or even a bobby pin or paper clip will do) to scrape off as much resin as you can.
3. If your piece can fit into a zip-top bag, fill the bag with some isopropyl alcohol (rubbing alcohol that can be picked up at the pharmacy) and some salt. Let it sit, checking every hour or so. Tough buildups may need to soak overnight; cleaner pieces may only need 1 to 3 hours or so. Note: If you're uncomfortable using alcohol, you can also use water and

lemon juice or check your local head shop for a cleaner specially made for cannabis supplies.

4. For bongs and bigger smoking devices, first disassemble the pieces. Then, using a large container, such as a cooking pot, or your sink, create a bath for your bong filled with isopropyl alcohol and salt, and submerge the whole thing (the smaller pieces, such as the bowl, can go in a zip-top bag).
5. When your glass supplies are looking sparkly and new, take them out of the soak. Rinse thoroughly with warm water to remove any remaining cleanser. Take a moment to marvel at your magical work.
6. Pack up your bowl to celebrate and get things dirty again. Clean regularly, once a week if possible, to prevent resin buildup and keep your supplies in tip-top shape.

30 MINUTES

Roll a Rose Blunt

Benefits: Homemade rose petal blunts are a beautiful alternative to traditional tobacco leaf blunts. In addition to being gorgeous, smoking rose petals is said to have calming and aphrodisiac properties that put you in touch with your physical body.

How does cannabis help? Cannabis will help you focus as you carefully handle the delicate rose petals. In addition, the enhanced senses of sight, smell, and taste that cannabis brings make rolling rose blunts an even more loving, romantic experience, whether you're practicing self-love or directing your love to another person.

HOW TO

1. Light up some cannabis and get focused. You're about to roll the most beautiful blunt you've ever smoked.
2. Pick up fresh roses. Consider the color. Red roses are associated with passion, pink roses with self-love and friendship, and yellow roses with sunshine and abundance. Choose a color that is aesthetically pleasing to you and that represents what you wish to manifest, from romantic love to joy to friendship.
3. Pull the petals off the roses. Then place the petals onto a baking tray.

4. Set your oven to broil. When it's ready, broil your petals until they turn a shade or two darker, about 10 seconds, then remove from the oven.
5. Lick the bottom of one of the petals and stick it to a second petal. Repeat for the remaining petal. You should have a line of three stuck-together petals that form a rose row resembling a rolling paper. Place the petals under the broiler for another 10 seconds to bind them to one another.
6. Remove the rose petals from the oven and let them rest to connect and cool off, about 2 minutes.
7. While your rose petals are cooling, grind your cannabis flower. Carefully scatter your ground bud along the middle of the rose petals as you would with a joint. Begin at one end and slowly tuck and wrap the rose petal over the cannabis, gently massaging the bud into place as you go. Be extra gentle as the rose petals are more delicate than rolling papers.
8. When you are finished rolling your rose blunt, place it under the broiler for 10 more seconds to help it set. Take it out, and let it rest for another 2 minutes, then break out your lighter and smoke your gorgeous rose blunt.

Reinvent Your Favorite Baked Treat

***Benefits*:** Baking edibles stimulates the senses, taps into creativity, and lets you share joy with others. Additionally, when you make your own cannabutter you can control the cannabis dosage and use the infused butter in your favorite treat.

How does cannabis help? Aside from acting as the superhero ingredient in the recipe, cannabis—especially if you use a sativa—helps keep you present, so the act of baking becomes an act of mindfulness. It also enhances your senses, so you better appreciate smell and taste (which also helps you become a better baker).

HOW TO

1. Inhale cannabis. Using the plant's tendency to stimulate your appetite, then ask yourself what treat sounds best to you. Is there a cookie you haven't had since childhood that would make a wonderful adult snack?
2. Preheat your oven to 240°F. Place ⅛ of an ounce of cannabis onto a nonstick baking sheet, cover with parchment paper, and bake for 30 to 45 minutes or until golden brown.
3. Remove the cannabis from the oven and set it aside to cool. Once cool to the touch, grind up the cannabis.
4. Combine 1 cup of water and 1 stick of unsalted butter in a medium-sized pot or saucepan. Let it simmer on low heat as the butter melts.

5. Stir in your ground cannabis. Keep the heat on a low simmer for 2 to 3 hours. Watch over it to ensure it doesn't boil and harm your precious ingredients.
6. When the mixture has cooled, strain the liquid cannabutter through a cheesecloth into a sealable container. Let the butter harden. Store it in the refrigerator for several weeks, or up to six months in the freezer. Should excess water form, drain it from the container.
7. Once your cannabutter has hardened, follow the recipe for your favorite baked treat, substituting cannabutter for the butter or oil called for in the original dish. Enjoy!

30 MINUTES

Go Shopping for Your Dream Pipe, Bong, or Bubbler

Benefits: Today's smoking devices are beautiful and elegant pieces of art. Connecting with and purchasing a smoking device that speaks to your aesthetic and lifestyle makes you more likely to use it to enhance your self-care routine.

How does cannabis help? Cannabis enhances your senses and your appreciation of art. What you smoke out of matters; it affects the onset of the high, the intensity, and how long it lasts. Use your heightened senses to listen to your body and select a smoking device which fits your needs.

HOW TO

1. While under the lovely influence of cannabis, research what smoking method speaks to you. Do you prefer the intensity of a bong? Would a discreet vaporizer work better with your lifestyle? Do you tend to smoke with friends? Maybe a crowd-pleasing bubbler would be a good fit? Create a mental shopping list before you head over to your local smoke shop.
2. Walk through the smoke shop and browse the merchandise. They may just be objects, but they are objects with a glorious purpose. Take your time selecting the tools that speak to you, then head home to enjoy your purchase and revel in the beautiful new object that you've chosen as part of your self-care routine.

AT LEAST 2 HOURS

Go to the Spa

Benefits: Massage reduces tension, pain, and stress. Facials keep your skin glowing and can also reduce stress, as can sitting in a steam room. Going to the spa tells your brain and body that you are not at work or home but in a place that allows you to focus solely on self-care.

How does cannabis help? The edibles used in this self-care activity last for a long time and are known for enhancing bodily sensations. Cannabis also helps you be present and focused on the touch rather than lost in thought.

HOW TO

1. Book an appointment and find safe transportation to and from the spa.
2. Once your spa day arrives, eat your edible of choice. Edibles take up to an hour and a half to kick in, so consume yours about an hour beforehand. When you arrive you will be feeling the early tingles of upliftment, which will blissfully increase during your time at the spa.
3. During your treatments, focus on the physical sensations that are happening. Notice the tension as it's rubbed out of your shoulders. Feel your face being polished. The sweat coming out of your body in the steam room. Let someone else take care of you.
4. Once you return home, rest your tended-to body, and continue to enjoy cannabis.

30 MINUTES

Plan Your Munchies Ahead of Time

Benefits: Preplanning snacks ensures your body is well fueled and ready to take on whatever your day has in store. It also ensures that you have a balanced range of options available to you when you need them.

How does cannabis help? Cannabis encourages appetite, which is excellent for those who need appetite stimulation. Considering what your body craves while in a heightened state will help you ensure your snacks are the ones best suited to your body's needs.

HOW TO

1. Embrace the munchies. Sit down somewhere you can write and enjoy cannabis without anyone bothering you.
2. Deeply inhale your cannabis and consider what your body is asking for. Do you have healthy options available that you can enjoy in an elevated state? For instance, you may love dried fruit, crackers and hummus, grapes, and dark chocolate.
3. Are there snacks that you crave but aren't "healthy," such as ice cream or nachos? Write these options down and don't feel bad about it! Just make sure your overall list is balanced and skews toward more healthy options overall.
4. After you've finished making your list, head to your local market to pick up your munchie supplies.

Take an Afternoon Nap

Benefits: Science shows us that naps can boost memory, mood, and job performance and reduce irritability. Regular naps also reduce stress and lower tension, which helps prevent heart disease.

How does cannabis help? Cannabis—especially indicas or high-CBD strains—is a known sleep aid. And edibles have a reputation as sleep medicine—due to their long-lasting nature, edibles help you not just fall asleep, but stay asleep.

HOW TO

1. Set a timer if needed and put away your phone.
2. Go somewhere in your home that invokes relaxation. Begin deep breathing, and consume cannabis as part of your breath by inhaling marijuana and exhaling its smoke. If you're opting for an edible, eat it prior, as they take an hour and a half to kick in.
3. Crawl under your covers. You deserve this nap. Get as fancy as you want. Try aromatherapy. Put on a sound machine. Wear earplugs or an eye mask. Do whatever you need to do to ensure that you're as comfortable as possible.
4. Close your eyes and allow the cannabis to transport you to the dream world. Practice deep breathing and drift off to sleep.
5. Wake up feeling refreshed and ready to tackle the rest of the day. If you need a pick-me-up try an active sativa.

Fully Inhabit Your Body

Benefits: When you're fully in your body, you're more grounded and more likely to make rational decisions. You're also more likely to be aware of what's happening in your body, from tension headaches to joint pain, and then be able to tend to yourself.

How does cannabis help? Cannabis helps you pause your worries. Fleeting thoughts and useless fears of the past or future are lost in the wind as cannabis heightens your physical senses and brings you fully into your body.

HOW TO

1. Find somewhere calm and quiet where you can set yourself up with a yoga mat, a blanket, or a pillow and your cannabis.
2. Get into lotus pose by sitting cross-legged on your yoga mat (or a blanket or pillow) and putting each foot on the opposite thigh. Then practice the fourfold breath by inhaling for 4 seconds, pausing for 4 seconds, exhaling for 4 seconds, and pausing for 4 seconds. Between rounds of breath, enjoy cannabis as desired.
3. When you feel that your body has been elevated, imagine that your bottom is attached to the ground by roots of a giant tree trunk that connect you to the Earth, cannabis, and every living thing.
4. Begin moving various parts of your body. Wiggle your toes. Bend forward to stretch. Is that built-up tension in your lower

back? Do some shoulder rolls. Check in for stiffness in your chest, which can be a sign of anxiety. Take additional hits of cannabis as desired. As thoughts or worries arise, allow them to float away like leaves in the wind. If it's important, it will come back to you. If it's just a worry, let it go. Cannabis has your back.

5. Notice as you allow yourself to sink fully into your body, inhabiting every inch of it, where it hurts and where it feels good. Feel the grounded energy of your body connected to the Earth.
6. When you're ready, get up and go about the rest of your day or evening, while holding onto the mindfulness gleaned. If you catch yourself disassociating, gently remind your head to drop back into the physical body so the two can operate at full function together.

15 MINUTES

Make a Cannabis Cocktail

Benefits: Drinking cannabis helps the body calm down and light up with euphoria, and this cannabis cocktail offers an alcohol alternative if you're looking to take a break from booze or give your favorite cocktail a creative spark.

How does cannabis help? Sipping on cannabis acts like a slowly consumed edible, inviting relaxation into the body.

HOW TO

1. Consider what type of a cocktail you want. Do you want to add cannabis to an alcoholic beverage? Maybe you could put a marijuana spin on a salty margarita. Do you want to try a new and exciting way to savor cannabis by adding it to a drink you typically have without the addition of this versatile herb? Maybe try something like healthy pineapple juice dosed with Pineapple Express cannabis strain?
2. Collect the supplies needed to create your cannabis cocktail, such as sparkling tonic, juices, and crushed ice.
3. Make your drink, then take out your cannabis tincture (see Create a Cannabis Tincture in Part 2).
4. Add your tincture to your drink being sure to dose responsibly based on your tolerance and if you are combining alcohol and cannabis.
5. Sip your drink and feel the cannabis begin to relax your body and invigorate your senses.

Create Your Own Incense

Benefits: Working with herbs is grounding and, depending on which herbs you choose to work with, the added aromatherapy will help your body feel either invigorated or serene. Creating your own incense leads to a sense of accomplishment; plus, now you have a new skill.

How does cannabis help? Cannabis acts as a focusing agent, which will help you attend to the task at hand: blending and crushing herbs. Marijuana will also heightens your sense of smell, so the qualities of whichever herbs you use will be intensified as they work their way into your body.

HOW TO

1. Enjoy cannabis in your form of choice. Once you're centered, enjoy a mental flipbook of smells—think sage, rose, cinnamon—and decide which incense you'd like to make. You can also get fancy and combine aromas to create your own signature incense. Keep your cannabis close throughout the process to use as needed.
2. Collect and lay out your supplies. You will need: a mortar and pestle, frosting tips for baking, wax paper, water, dried herbs of your choosing, cannabis, makko powder, and a lighter. Such items can be found in baking and natural food stores, or easily ordered online.
3. Mindfully crush your dried herbs using a mortar and pestle. Feel the pestle as it crushes the herbs, releasing their aroma

into the air. Consciously take a deep breath and let the calming or invigorating properties of the herbs you've chosen act on your body.

4. In a bowl combine makko powder, a binding agent that helps with combustion, with the ground herbs. This tree bark additive should be mixed in using one part makko to three parts herb.
5. Begin adding water as you continue to mix. When your creation becomes hard enough that you can mold it with your hands, take the incense out of the bowl and place it on top of the wax paper. Then knead it until it becomes firm enough to resemble cookie dough.
6. Begin to form the mixture into small cones. You can do this fairly casually using the corner of the wax paper, or if you want something more defined, use a frosting tip used for icing.
7. Place your cones on a fresh piece of wax paper and leave them alone to fully dry. Depending on your climate, this will take 12 hours to one week.
8. When your incense is ready light it up along with a joint, and enjoy the effects that the aromatherapy and cannabis have on your body.

15 MINUTES

Make a Grocery List

Benefits: Planning your trip to the grocery store ahead of time ensures that you will have on hand exactly what you need in your kitchen, both in terms of healthy options that nourish your body and treats that excite your taste buds.

How does cannabis help? Cannabis stimulates the appetite and helps you get in touch with what you've been craving. Making your list under the influence of marijuana's creative properties is an adventure that nourishes your body and excites your love of food.

HOW TO

1. Grab a notebook, a pen, and your cannabis. Take a few deep breaths and hits of cannabis to help you relax and stimulate your appetite.
2. Once you start to feel hungry, ask yourself if there are foods your body is craving. When was the last time you had fresh veggies? Are you in need of protein? Let your body tell you what it needs and write down what it says.
3. If an idea for a dish comes to mind and you aren't sure of all the ingredients, explore recipes on your computer or phone and add those ingredients to your list.
4. Before you take your list to the store, check it over and make sure you wrote down all the essentials, such as coffee, milk, pet food, and cooking oils to make sure your pantry will be stocked with what your body needs.

Explore Your Erogenous Zones

Benefits: Self-touch, especially when coupled with orgasm, reduces stress, aids in sleep, and helps you relax and gain self-confidence. Exploring erogenous zones outside of the genitalia, such as nipples, scalp, neck, arms, and feet, teaches you the many ways your body feels pleasure so you can find a personalized self-love practice.

How does cannabis help? Cannabis can increase blood flow, heighten pleasure, and decrease discomfort in your erogenous zones. The plant gives these benefits when inhaled, along with a nice high. You can enhance these effects by doubling down and adding a cannabis topical, which provides localized, non-psychoactive pain relief and anti-inflammatory benefits.

HOW TO

1. When it comes to self-touch and the erogenous zones, everyone is different. Perhaps you want to give yourself a foot massage using a cannabis topical, or maybe you want to masturbate to see how an orgasm feels in your enhanced mindset. Grab your cannabis and get comfy in conjunction with what you desire. Is an uplifted orgasm the goal? Settle into bed. Are you working on tensions in the neck from typing? Sit down on a yoga mat.
2. Either naked or in comfortable clothing, depending on your desires, begin by enjoying cannabis. Edibles are the gold star of body highs, but you'll need to plan ahead because it can

take up to an hour and a half to feel their effects. For immediate results smoke a joint or hit a vape until you feel delightful.

3. Relax and begin to get in touch with your body. Using your hands, a personal massager, and/or a cannabis topical (if you're touching your genitals, companies such as Foria make cannabis-infused pleasure sprays), take your time as you explore your body.
4. Notice what feels good. Is there an area on your genitals that's gone previously unnoticed? Is there a cramp in your neck you didn't notice before? Attend to your needs. Revel in the power that you can pleasure yourself on your own.
5. When you finish, regardless of whether you enjoyed a foot rub or erotic touch, jot down what felt good so you can enjoy it again. And, if you brought yourself to orgasm, how did it feel from an elevated mind-set? Was the intensity heightened? How did engaging in this intimate act of physical self-care feel?

Create Your Own Topical

Benefits: Creating your own cannabis topical allows you to manage the dose and quantity of cannabis. You can tailor the entire product to your needs, from the fragrance to the consistency, and even the packaging, to ensure that your finished product is perfect for you and your body.

How does cannabis help? Creating a cannabis topical under the influence of the herb helps you let your guard down so you can get messy and experiment with textures and essential oil scents. Opt for a sativa to keep your mind on point and concentrated on the physicality of the luxurious task at hand.

HOW TO

1. To begin, center yourself with a hit of cannabis. A vape is an easy intake method to have around while completing manual projects.
2. Collect your ingredients. You'll need roughly 10 grams of cannabis, a nonstick baking sheet, parchment paper, a grinder or mortar and pestle, ⅓ cup of olive oil, 1½ cups of coconut oil, a double boiler (or a makeshift one with a pot placed on top of a pot), a cheesecloth, ⅓ cup of beeswax, and essential oils of your choosing.
3. Preheat your oven to 245°F. Place your cannabis on a nonstick baking sheet, cover with parchment paper, and bake for 30 to 45 minutes or until golden brown.
4. Remove the cannabis from the oven and set it aside to cool.

5. Add the olive oil and coconut oil in the double boiler. Stir at a low temperature for roughly 25 minutes, then add your decarboxylated ground cannabis to the oil mixture and continue stirring for another 25 minutes.
6. Move your creation away from the flames and filter out the cannabis buds using a cheesecloth, leaving only infused oil.
7. Combine the infused oil and the beeswax in the double boiler. Add essential oil as desired (I like to use 6–8 drops, but this is a personal decision). Cinnamon oil is spicy and seductive. Lavender is calm and soothing. Orange awakens the senses. Use your high mind: What does your body need?
8. When everything is combined, remove from the heat. Let your body potion cool off, and apply to your body as needed. Feel the cannabis soak into your skin and begin working its nourishing and anti-inflammatory properties to ease aches and pains as your skin glows. Store the topical in a sealable jar for up to a year.

Stretch

Benefits: Stretching increases flexibility, improves blood flow to muscles, and helps relax your body and mind. It helps to improve your posture, your physical performance, and can even both heal and prevent back pain.

How does cannabis help? Cannabis helps you inhabit your body, relax your muscles, and be fully present in the moment. It reduces pain without numbing you to the point of being susceptible to injury. The psychoactive effects of cannabis also aid in pain visualization and body awareness so you understand where attention is needed.

HOW TO

1. Sit on a yoga mat somewhere quiet with enough space to move. If you like, put on music that helps you melt into relaxation.
2. Begin breathing by inhaling cannabis and exhaling tension. Feel your body start to relax.
3. Every body is different, so while listening to yours, begin stretching. Roll your neck, touch your toes, and flex your ankles.
4. Use your high state of mind to visualize each area of tightness or soreness, and adjust your stretching accordingly. Keep your cannabis topical nearby to apply to any painful areas as needed.
5. Once your body is thoroughly stretched and relaxed, bookend the session by sitting for a few moments alternating deep breathing with cannabis inhalation.

2 HOURS

Enjoy an After-Dinner Joint

Benefits: Sitting or standing upright, rather than lying down, prevents acid reflux post dinner, and engaging in this self-care ritual by taking a walk after a meal will aid in digestion, improve your mood, and boost your metabolism.

How does cannabis help? Cannabis supports healthy digestion and can alleviate symptoms of many digestive problems, including acid reflux, nausea, and diarrhea. As you relax and unwind with an after-dinner joint, the calming effects of cannabis will help your body process your meal.

HOW TO

1. If you ate dinner by yourself, go ahead and settle down to reward yourself for taking care of your body. Sit upright to encourage healthy digestion and to prevent acid reflux; reflect on how delicious your dinner was, and how thankful you are for the joy in your life. Feel the fullness in your stomach and be aware of and grateful for the food that is fueling your body. And if you are experiencing tummy troubles, get comfy and use the cannabis to help alleviate them.
2. If you're with friends, offer to share a joint. Is everyone versed on joint etiquette? Puff, puff, pass is real. Everyone can take two puffs and then pass it to the next person. Enjoy watching your loved ones get high and laugh and tell stories. This is a powerful time to bond with intimates, just as you would over after-dinner drinks.

3. Once you've chilled out for a bit and you can feel your food digesting in your body, go on a brief stroll. Bring along a joint or vape pen. Ideally after-dinner walks should take place 30 minutes after you finished eating and last 15 to 20 minutes.
4. When you're ready, take advantage of marijuana's appetite-stimulating properties and treat yourself (and your friends) by indulging in a fabulous dessert.

A WEEKEND

Take a Staycation

***Benefits*:** Rest is crucial for both your physical and mental health. Just taking a weekend break will help relieve stress and increase your creativity.

How does cannabis help? Cannabis helps you let go to settle into your staycation, and lighting up can turn your home into a resort. Certain strains, especially heavy indicas, promote full-body highs for relaxing and sleeping. Marijuana can act as your nurse during your staycation by fighting migraines, cramps, anxiety, and other physical afflictions.

HOW TO

1. Mark a weekend in your calendar. Ensure you have no work to do, nowhere to be that isn't fun and relaxing, and that your home is clean and well stocked with food and cannabis. Long-lasting edibles, stimulating sativas, relaxing indicas, and pain-relieving topicals can all become a part of your staycation.
2. Unsure of what you need during your staycation? Light up, sit down with an elevated state of mind, and meditate to listen to what your body and mind says. Give yourself permission to do nothing. Or perhaps you want to catch up on a television show. Do you want to hang out with your pets? Or nap all day? Have you been so busy that you miss cooking, or do you just want a pizza delivered to your door? This is your staycation; plan it according to what you need. The only rule is that

you must treat your staycation like an actual vacation and not work.

3. If you want company, invite your partner or friend over. If you need to get out of the house, explore your town or city as you would if you were a tourist. Invite a friend or partner and go to places and events that you usually take for granted because you live there. Cannabis turns sightseeing into exploration due to its sensory enhancement.
4. Relax, rest, enjoy cannabis, and revel in your staycation. By the time Monday rolls around you'll be refreshed and renewed.

AT LEAST 15 MINUTES

Give Cannabis Kisses

Benefits**:** Kissing someone reduces stress, anxiety, and blood pressure and can boost your immune system. Making out also bonds you with your partner and floods your body and brain with the euphoric chemicals oxytocin, dopamine, and serotonin.

How does cannabis help? A cannabis kiss is when you consensually blow smoke into your partner's mouth and get one another high by kissing. Cannabis, which has been used as an aphrodisiac across cultures and centuries due to THC's mood-enhancing and activating properties, allows you to connect with a partner in a lavish and sensual new way. If you're anxiety-prone a calming strain high in CBD is the best aphrodisiac option to relieve any insecurities.

HOW TO

1. Light up your joint, then very carefully place the lit end into your mouth making sure not to burn your lips or mouth. The end that you suck on should be facing away from you, backward compared to how you normally use a joint.
2. Lean in toward your partner. As they open their mouth, make contact, so the joint butt goes inside their mouth. Blow. A stream of smoke will pour from your mouth and into theirs, entering their lungs and giving them a powerful hit of cannabis combined with a human connection.

3. If you don't feel comfortable placing the lit end of a joint in your mouth, try the alternative. Simply take a big hit of cannabis using your smoking device of choice. Lean into your partner and blow the smoke out of your mouth into theirs. This is technically secondhand smoke and may be less effective at getting them high, but it still works and the delivery can be highly arousing.
4. Ask your partner to return the favor, and enjoy this act of physical self-care.

AT LEAST 20 MINUTES

Try a Body Scan

Benefits: Body scans, where you mindfully scan your entire body looking for discomfort, bring you out of your head and into your body. Once you pay close attention to how your body feels, you can note where pain lies and treat it appropriately.

How does cannabis help? Performing a body scan with an elevated mind helps you to not only focus on your body but to better feel and visualize any pain you're experiencing. Additionally, cannabis topicals, which are used after the body scan, provide non-psychoactive pain relief by reducing inflammation and treating soreness and pain locally.

HOW TO

1. Create a nest where your body would like to be for your body scan. Light candles and stretch out on a yoga mat, snuggle into a fluffy blanket, or sit on a beautiful cushion—whatever makes your body happy. Place your cannabis, both your method of inhalation and your topical, nearby.
2. Take a hit. For a few minutes simply inhale and exhale to get into a meditative state. As you inhale and exhale with cannabis, feel the floor supporting your body. You don't have to worry about doing any work because gravity is doing it for you. Relax into your body.
3. Once you're entirely focused on your body, begin the body scan. Start with your head. Do you have a headache? Move onto your neck and shoulders. Do they feel tense and tight?

4. Continue the body scan mindfully, noting where any pain is hiding, until you get to your toes. How are your feet? Are they sore from carrying you around all day? Thank your feet for holding you up.
5. Take your time and gently sit back up. Rub your cannabis or CBD topical into any areas that are sore, stiff, or uncomfortable. Then, as much as you can, relax and rest your body as the cannabis works its magic.

30 MINUTES

Make a Face Mask

Benefits: The ingredients in this face mask moisturize, remove dead skin, unclog and tighten pores, reduce dark spots, and firm the skin.

How does cannabis help? The psychoactive properties of cannabis, especially indicas, edibles, and high-CBD strains, relieve stress and anxiety to help your body relax. And cannabis topicals contain anti-inflammatory and antioxidant properties for the skin.

HOW TO

1. Gather half an avocado, 1 teaspoon of plain yogurt, 1 teaspoon of honey, a lemon wedge, and ½ teaspoon of cannabis tincture. A tincture made with alcohol is fine for oily skin, but coconut oil is best for dry skin (see Create a Cannabis Tincture in Part 2).
2. In a mixing bowl, smash the avocado with a spoon. Add the yogurt and honey and squeeze the lemon slice, carefully removing any seeds. Add cannabis tincture. Stir until the mixture is goopy.
3. Wash your face, put on the mask, and light up a joint. Smoking a joint typically takes roughly the same time as a face mask takes to dry, so cover your skin care and cannabis consumption needs simultaneously. When you finish the joint, rinse off the mask, and enjoy your clean skin and the buzz of the cannabis.

Exercise

Benefits: Light exercise such as a walk, a restorative yoga class, or some cardio on a stationary bike can build and maintain bone and muscle strength, reduce your risk of disease, improve skin through the release of antioxidants, and aid in memory and brain health. Exercise releases endorphins and provides a mood boost.

How does cannabis help? Cannabis turns exercise from a chore into an endorphin-boosting thrill. It keeps you aware of your bodily sensations while reducing pain. Like exercise on its own cannabis boosts your mood and releases endorphins, so combining the two will leave you feeling motivated to perform this self-care activity.

HOW TO

1. Put on your workout gear, stretch, and smoke up while listening to your favorite music to get in the zone.
2. Choose a light, low-risk exercise to try. A walk in the park? A bike ride on the gym's stationary? An easy yoga or pilates class at the gym or at home? Try an activity that's accessible for you. But be careful; since marijuana can affect balance, now is not the time for martial arts or any exercise involving challenging yoga poses or heavy weights. Opt for something soothing and low risk. Our bodies need restorative motion as much as they need to be pushed to advanced training routines.

3. Once you're at your exercise location use your high to notice how your body responds, which joints are tight, and how good it feels to break a sweat. Take advantage of the inhibition-mitigating dopamine rush from cannabis to let your guard down and stop worrying about what you look like working out.
4. Let marijuana's mind-expanding properties take your workout to the next level. Are you on a stroll, or are you a spy scoping out a new neighborhood and taking in every detail? Are you on a stationary bike, or riding through the mountains to metal music? Do you finally see why yoga is a moving meditation and not just a fitness practice?
5. When you're ready, end the workout, sit down with some more cannabis, and don't forget to hydrate and stretch (see Stretch in this part). Apply your cannabis topical to areas experiencing muscle pain.

AT LEAST 30 MINUTES

Cuddle with Someone You Love

Benefits: Cuddling is good for heart health as it can lower blood pressure and decrease stress in addition to bringing you closer to your partner. The brain releases oxytocin during cuddling, which both facilitates bonding and encourages sound sleep.

How does cannabis help? Studies show cannabis helps you feel gratitude toward your partner and strengthens your physical connection. Cannabis also heightens the physical sensation of touch, so expect a highly sensual cuddle session.

HOW TO

1. Whether you're snuggling and watching a movie or in bed after sex, make time to connect physically with your partner.
2. Light up and share the cannabis. Relinquish control as the cannabis disinhibits you, so you feel comfortable opening up emotionally with your partner.
3. With your bodies touching, check in on one another. If sex was involved, ask questions such as, "Was that good for you? What could I do better next time? What did you like about it?" and of course, "Can I get you anything to eat or drink?"
4. Use your elevated mind to appreciate your bodies and the way you fit together. Let love in.
5. Snuggling doesn't have to be linked to sex. It works as a form of physical connection on its own. Use this opportunity to connect emotionally. Catch up on your partner's work life and general well-being. Make sure they feel happy and secure with

how your relationship is evolving. Ensure that the communication is a two-way street.

6. Use your heightened awareness to make use of all your senses: Inhale your partner's scent. Admire how beautiful they are in your arms. Kiss them and notice how they taste. Listen to their heartbeat and the inhales and exhales of their breathing.
7. Share more cannabis together until you reach a pleasurable state you're comfortable in.

Make a CBD Smoothie

Benefits: Smoothies offer on-the-go nutrition, and this energy-boosting, nutrient-dense CBD smoothie is packed full of vitamins A, B, and C and potassium, as well as protein, fiber, and omega-3 fatty acids. These nutrients keep your body strong, active, and working at its highest level.

How does cannabis help? CBD, especially full-spectrum CBD made from the whole flowering cannabis plant, reduces anxiety and stress, and acts as an anti-inflammatory. It binds to the receptors in your endocannabinoid system, which regulates everything from the central nervous system and chronic pain to mood disorders and cancer.

HOW TO

1. Get your groceries to make a CBD green smoothie. You will need 1 banana, 2 cups of kale, 2 cups of chopped pineapple, 2 cups of coconut water, 2 tablespoons of chia seeds, and 2 ml of CBD oil.
2. Unpeel the banana, remove the stems from the kale, and chop the pineapple (or use frozen pineapple). Place the banana, kale, pineapple, and coconut water into a blender and puree on high until smooth, about 30 to 45 seconds. Add the chia seeds and CBD oil and pulse for a few rounds to combine.
3. Pour your smoothie into a glass and enjoy this energizing and nutrient-rich drink and all it has to offer.

Experiment with Edibles

***Benefits*:** While edibles are marvelous when dosed correctly, too much can lead to paranoia, hallucinations, and just feeling "too high." Eating too much won't hurt you, but it can be uncomfortable. Everyone has different tolerance levels, so using a weekend to learn your correct dosage allows you to experiment in a space you feel safe in, in addition to offering rest and stress relief and a good dose of physical self-care.

How does cannabis help? Edibles are perfect when you want an elevated state of mind for an extended period, such as a weekend off, but don't want to have to worry about keeping cannabis on you. They're also fantastic for pain relief and insomnia. Learning your right dosage allows you to reap these benefits without the negative side effects.

HOW TO

1. Clear your schedule for an entire weekend and invite over someone you trust who also enjoys cannabis. If you have the means consider renting a cabin in nature.
2. Procure your edibles from your local dispensary or make your own (see Reinvent Your Favorite Baked Treat in this part). And make sure you have plenty of food and fun movies to watch.
3. Keep CBD around. CBD counteracts the effects of THC and can be used to lower a high should you overindulge. If you take too much THC, have some CBD tincture and remember that this will fade and you cannot overdose from cannabis.

4. Try an edible that contains 5 mg of cannabis, which is the amount suggested as a starting dose. Remember edibles take about an hour and a half to kick in, so don't eat anymore until 2 hours have passed to be safe.
5. If 2 hours have passed and you don't feel much, try 10 mg. Increase your consumption in 5 mg intervals, giving yourself 2 hours in between, until you find the edible dosage that's right for you. Keep in mind that everyone reacts differently to edibles. For some people, 5 mg is plenty; others can function just fine after consuming 50 mg.
6. When you are at a happy high, enjoy it! Hang out with your friend, tell stories, goof around, eat some snacks, and put on a movie. If you're up for it, enjoy a stroll outside.
7. Congratulations on finding a safe dosage that works for you. Be aware that tolerance fluctuates. Continue to adjust as needed throughout your lifetime to enjoy the benefits of edibles without the negative side effects.

AN HOUR (OR AS LONG AS YOU LIKE!)

Hang Out Naked

Benefits: Everyone struggles with body insecurities. Combat this ingrained societal body shame and become comfortable in your body by spending time naked alone.

How does cannabis help? Cannabis lower inhibitions. It's also an herb of acceptance. The plant aids in emotionally processing, which helps you understand and accept other people, as well as yourself and your body.

HOW TO

1. When you're home alone and ready to feel free, put on music that makes you happy and confident.
2. Set yourself up somewhere comfy and inhale, ingest, or vape away until you're delightfully high. It's just you here. No one else is around. If you're wary of being naked the dopamine rush of cannabis will help lower inhibitions and anxiety and help you feel comfortable in your own skin.
3. In your own time, shed your clothes. Take your time, removing piece by piece, and let the music and cannabis boost your self-confidence until you're totally naked.
4. It may feel strange for a minute, but accept that. Let yourself feel the hard emotions. When we don't feel emotions, we bottle them up. So allow yourself to feel insecure. Sit with those feelings. Compare them to reality. You are beautiful. You are an entire complex human. Everyone feels insecure about their bodies.

5. Try having some fun, dancing a bit, or kick back on the couch with snacks and your favorite TV show. Tap into the power that comes with being free of clothes.
6. Consume more cannabis and notice the good things about your body. Does the way your hair falls down your spine feel good? Do you like how your butt jiggles to the music? What about how your collarbone feels when caressed? Use your enlightened state to notice all that's good with the beautiful body you were born into.
7. Continue to have fun consuming cannabis while naked until you're tuckered out, then get dressed or curl up under a blanket to rest.

PART 2

Mind

30 MINUTES

Try Journaling

***Benefits*:** Writing out your emotions can help you process them, and laying out your concerns can lead to a solution and fight depression, anxiety, and stress. Journals also act as a time capsule. Years from now, look back and marvel at all that you've experienced.

How does cannabis help? Adding cannabis to this practice increases creativity in your writing and aids in emotional processing. Harness the creative power of cannabis by lighting up and then putting pen to paper without fear of judgment.

HOW TO

1. Pick up a brand-new journal in a style that brings you joy.
2. Find somewhere cozy to settle in with your cannabis, journal, and pen, then enjoy some cannabis. As your mind opens, flip through the new journal. Instead of stressing over each blank page, understand that you have an entire future ahead of you with which to fill those pages. Relish the hope the future holds.
3. If you have journals from your past, take a moment to peek through them. Use your uplifted mind to reflect on the passage of time. Look back on all that you've survived, lived through, and accomplished. Know that this fresh new journal represents all the colorful life experiences ahead of you.
4. Enjoy another hit, and take a moment to pause and check in with yourself. Are you stressed? Jealous? Loved? Afraid?

Take all those thoughts, emotions, and concerns and get them out of your head and onto the paper. Just start writing. It's okay if it doesn't follow a timeline. It's okay if your handwriting is sloppy and your grammar isn't perfect. This is for you and only you. Write about what's happening in your life, write out any fears, and celebrate yourself by recording any accomplishments.

5. When you finish journaling, take a moment to enjoy cannabis again and do another mental check-in. How do you feel? Are any situations clearer now that they've been written out? Does your hard work feel more valid now that it's spelled out with pen and paper? Do you feel lighter after taking your worries out of your head, and has their power over you been diminished by describing them on the pages of your journal?
6. Work on integrating journaling into your daily life, ideally at the end of the day before bedtime.

ABOUT AN HOUR OF ACTIVE COOKING TIME, BUT A MONTH TO FULLY FORM

Create a Cannabis Tincture

Benefits: Creating your own tincture gets you up close and personal with the plant to experience its touch, taste, and smell in a productive method. Making a psychoactive tincture out of fresh buds is a form of alchemy that facilitates mental focus and patience.

How does cannabis help? Cannabis aids in cognitive function to help even those who aren't at home in the kitchen to create a magic potion. It also helps you bring your creative properties to the foreground as you experiment.

HOW TO

1. Collect your ingredients. You will need 1 ounce of cannabis shake, or loose leftover cannabis crumbles (Note: You can collect shake over time or buy some at a dispensary.); 2 cups of high-proof alcohol such as Everclear or 151 rum, or 2 cups coconut oil if you prefer to avoid alcohol; a mason jar; tincture bottles; and a strainer.
2. Connect with cannabis and enjoy a puff or two before you begin.
3. Preheat your oven to 245°F. Place your cannabis on a non-stick baking sheet, cover with parchment paper, and bake for 30 to 45 minutes or until golden brown.
4. Remove the cannabis from the oven and set it aside to cool. Once cool to the touch, grind the cannabis to a fine crumble.
5. Fill your mason jar with your high-proof alcohol or oil and your decarboxylated ground cannabis. Seal the lid.

6. Let it sit for a month, shaking once a day. (Bonus points for dancing while shaking!)
7. After a month, your tincture will be ready. Strain the liquid tincture through coffee filters into a wide-mouthed container.
8. Carefully fill tincture containers with your potion and store indefinitely in a sealed container in a cool and dark environment. Use when needed.

Prepare for Difficult Situations

Benefits: Preparing for a difficult situation allows you to consider the worst-case scenario and compare it to other adversities you've faced and triumphed over to raise your confidence. Pausing before reacting also gives you time to replace worry with rational thought.

How does cannabis help? Cannabis offers perspective when things seem more difficult than they actually are. It can help you feel good about yourself and will help calm your mind as you prepare for any potentially emotionally wrought interactions.

HOW TO

1. Sit down somewhere quiet away from interruption. Bring a pillow or your yoga mat and your cannabis.
2. For a few minutes, sit in the silence and close your eyes.
3. Take a few enhanced inhales and exhales by inhaling cannabis and exhaling the smoke or vapor. Keep it relaxed and casual.
4. Once you feel calmer, ask your brain what's going on. Are you dealing with jealousy in a relationship and it's time to have a talk? Are you considering leaving your job? Do you have to see family who stress you out? While maintaining a steady breath, imagine the worst possible outcome. What could happen? A breakup? An uncomfortable few days? A period of financial stress?
5. Gain some perspective by being brutally honest with yourself. You've already lived through and survived most of those

worst-case scenarios, haven't you? You're stronger than you think.

6. Now, using the mind-expanding properties of cannabis, consider: What if the best possible outcome occurs? What if the relationship talk goes well, or you reunite with old family and feel joy, or you make a career change that leads to greater happiness? Visualize your best-case scenario coming to life.
7. Now visualize a protective aura emanating from you. Know that you are safe. If a difficult situation leads to hardships, it's nothing that you can't handle. However, why not project positivity and give assuming the best a shot?
8. When you finish the meditation, take another toke or two and see how you feel. Do you feel calmer, like you've got this, and might even come out on the other side for the better?

Create an Inspired Vision Board

Benefits: Visualization can lead to manifestation. When you create a physical visual reminder of your desires, especially one that you put time and effort into, you'll be inspired to make the moves needed to accomplish those dreams.

How does cannabis help? Cannabis aids in creativity and asks you to dream big. Using cannabis while creating a vision board not only makes the activity more fun but produces a more fruitful outcome, as you are more likely to use your imagination.

HOW TO

1. Pick up your supplies. To create a vision board, you will need old magazines; scissors; tape, glue, or pushpins; and something to attach everything to, such as poster board, a scrapbook, or a bulletin board.
2. Gather your cannabis, and set up shop somewhere with plenty of room where it's okay to make a mess.
3. Take a moment to tap into yourself, and consume some cannabis. As your mind opens, ask yourself what you want out of your life. Is there a professional field that you're looking to break into? What about a city that you want to visit? Are you ready to settle down and want to attract an ideal life partner? Perhaps you are in need of self-love and want to create a vision board that celebrates you and reminds you to love yourself.

4. Set the mood. Use music and lighting to create the vibe you wish to invoke. Perhaps if it's a vision board about a job you can play music that makes you feel professionally powerful, and if it's for travel, contains songs that remind you of that place.
5. Begin crafting. Using cannabis as you please, cut, glue, pin, collage, and make a grand mess while creating the vision board of your dreams. Cut out photos and quotes, form words from letters, and don't be afraid to get creative and weird. As you create your board, visualize your dreams coming to life.
6. When your board is ready, hang it up where you can see it every day. All the hard work that you put in will help remind you of your goals, and will help you turn those dreams into reality through the power of manifestation. Never forget that there is magic in boldness. If other people can make their dreams come true so can you.

30 MINUTES

Paint, Color, Sketch, or Doodle for Calm

Benefits: Creating art has miraculous side effects. Mentally, it sharpens memory, aids in problem-solving, and helps with recall abilities (research shows that art therapy benefits people with Alzheimer's disease). Emotionally, artistic pursuits relieve stress and open us up to the deepest range of emotional experience.

How does cannabis help? The long-standing relationship between cannabis and art demonstrates that the herb facilitates creative abilities, encourages self-expression, and helps increase artistic productivity. Cannabis, especially strains high in CBD, relieves stress, and stress can inhibit creativity. Combine cannabis and art for a two-punch dose of calm.

HOW TO

1. Set up your art supplies somewhere that encourages inspiration, then indulge in cannabis. As the high expands your mind, glance down at your paper and imagine the page filling with your work.
2. Begin drawing. It doesn't have to be anything more than a doodle. Give yourself permission to let your mind and hand wander.
3. Step back and observe what you have created. Is it a drawing that releases old trauma? An image dedicated to a goal you wish to accomplish? There's no right or wrong way to create art; however, reflecting on what came out of your expanded mind can help you understand your inner needs and intensify this mental self-care activity.

10 MINUTES

Create a Cannabis-on-the-Go Kit

Benefits: Creating your own cannabis-on-the-go kit allows you to personalize what you need for a night out based on your cannabis use and lifestyle.

How does cannabis help? Cannabis stimulates cognitive function and encourages creative problem-solving. Lighting up to create your cannabis-on-the-go kit helps you come up with unique and effective ways to store your medicine and personalize your mental self-care.

HOW TO

1. Light up and reflect upon your lifestyle. Think about what you need. A smell-proof case of prerolled joints to bring to parties? All your joint-rolling supplies handily stashed in a pocket-sized container? A small bag to hold your vaporizer and a few edibles?
2. Choose a carry case that speaks to your lifestyle and will be easy to take along with you for a night out. If you're using edibles, it can be a bag or box of treats, but return them to your fridge or freezer after going out. If you prefer inhalation, use a clutch bag that will fit inside your purse or pocket. If you're worried about the smell of flowers, you can buy cases made for traveling with cannabis at head shops across the country or online.
3. Next, pack your bag. If you enjoy cannabis flowers, you'll need cannabis, a small jar or container, a lighter, and a one-hitter

pipe or rolling papers. A small metal stick or pipe cleaners, available at any craft store or online, are useful for those using pipes.

4. Storing the cannabis is the most crucial part. Pill bottles work for short-term use, but it's ill-advised to leave your flower in there for extended periods. Cannabis buds need to be kept in an airtight container at room temperature to avoid either becoming overly moist or too dried out. Various mini containers and jars are available online.
5. Place your on-the-go kit somewhere safe near your purse or keys (an area where you will be sure to pass by before going out) and rest easy knowing that, whenever you head out, you have what you need ready to go.

AN HOUR

Pick Up a New Instrument

Benefits: Research shows that playing music strengthens cognitive abilities, such as memory and mental processing time. Creating music can also aid in your ability to multitask. The activity can reduce stress, and one study demonstrates that playing music even reduces anxiety and depression levels.

How does cannabis help? Cannabis heightens your senses and therefore will enhance your appreciation for the beautiful sounds you create. Relaxing with an indica can allow you to let loose and jam; sativa strains can improve mental focus, which can help you learn new things.

HOW TO

1. Choose the instrument you'd like to learn. Do you have rusty skills with guitar or keyboard that you'd like to pick up again? Perhaps your instrument is your voice and you just want to start practicing singing along to your favorite songs. If you don't have an instrument, and buying one is out of your budget, use a music app like GarageBand on your computer or phone to electronically create your own beats and music—and remember that there is always your voice, which is free. Once you've decided on what makes sense for you, gather your musical supplies.
2. With music playing, take your cannabis. As your mind elevates notice how the songs become richer. Imagine yourself as a rock star, playing the song to thousands of screaming fans.

Go with a song that makes you happy and that you genuinely want to learn to play.

3. When you're ready, prepare your keyboard, guitar, digital device, or voice, and pick up any songbook or music you found online and start playing. Keep your cannabis next to you and partake as desired.
4. Let loose and jam out. Allow the cannabis to carry away any worries or thoughts about how you sound or self-criticisms if you mess up. Remember that the goal is not to be perfect. Instead have some fun, make some noise, be creative, and enjoy this mental self-care exercise.

Go on a Cannabis-Friendly Outing

Benefits: Activities that take you outside have profound effects on your mental well-being by lowering stress levels and increasing happiness. Whether you're with friends, a date, or enjoying a day alone, sometimes you want a break from the bar scene. Appreciate a cannabis-friendly outing, such as going to the botanical garden or an amusement park.

How does cannabis help? Incorporating cannabis into an adventure where you wouldn't normally experience a high is a self-care activity that asks you to step out of your comfort zone and try something new. By intensifying senses, cannabis turns the mundane into a whole new world.

HOW TO

1. Begin by brainstorming what you would like to do. Is there a park or beach nearby where you can have a picnic? Maybe you'd love to experience the adrenaline rush of an amusement park or the mental stimulation of a museum when indulging in cannabis? Plan a day, afternoon, or evening that cannabis would help set apart from your traditional routine.
2. Before you head out on your adventure, indulge in cannabis. Note that edibles work perfectly for this activity, because they can be taken beforehand and last a long time. Should you want to bring them with you and take more cannabis while you're out, you don't have to worry about smoking or vaping around plants or animals.

3. Meet up with your friends or partner, or fly solo, and head out for your planned activity using a safe mode of transportation (so you don't have to worry about driving).
4. When you get to your destination, notice how cannabis increases your senses. Does the smell of nature feel more pronounced? Are colors brighter and rays of sunshine more powerful? Can you hear the voices of other humans, or rustling leaves, or wildlife? If you're drinking a beverage or have packed a picnic, notice how cannabis enhances taste. Respect the rules of your destination of choice, but if you can, run your hands through the grass, or stream, and even your own hair and skin. Notice how the sun feels warming your body.
5. When you get home, reflect on the experience and how fulfilling this self-care activity was for you.

AT LEAST AN HOUR

Do Your Chores

Benefits: Once you clean up, any stress regarding overdue chores is swept away with the dirt.

How does cannabis help? Mundane tasks feel like fun craft projects when done with a heightened mind. For example, washing dishes isn't a chore, but an opportunity to play with bubbles. If you need an energy boost to keep you motivated, opt for a sativa or a high-THC strain.

HOW TO

1. Consume cannabis, then tackle your chores one by one. Focus on the pleasure in each activity. Watch the bathtub turn from grimy to sparkling clean with the help of your hand, soap, and a sponge. Make your bed and notice how cozy it looks. Enjoy the knowledge that later on you'll get to crawl into that comfortable bed.
2. Consider yourself a magician and cannabis your secret weapon. You aren't doing chores, but transforming a space. Your vacuum becomes a friendly robot ready to clear away unhealthy dirt.
3. Sit back and admire your hard work. Try a healing indica high in CBD to unwind and rest.

AT LEAST 15 MINUTES

Create a Calming Playlist

Benefits: Music can change your entire mood, and a calming playlist can help you relax, decompress, or get work done. Create one ahead of time, learning new music as you go, so all you have to do to get in the zone is press play when you want to chill.

How does cannabis help? Cannabis heightens your sense of hearing, enhancing sound awareness and therefore musical appreciation. Creating a playlist with a lifted mind will help you select the best tracks to induce a meditative mind-set, as cannabis (especially sativas) improves focus.

HOW TO

1. Relax with some cannabis. Allow the herb to calm your mind. Then open whatever music streaming app you use on your computer or phone. Let the cannabis speak to you. What keeps you calm? Create a playlist with the title of your choice for your favorite chill songs.
2. If you need help selecting songs, most streaming services offer relaxing or focusing playlists with ambient music. Put one on, adding songs that you like, and learning about new artists that speak to you.
3. When you're finished, indulge in some more cannabis and start your playlist from the beginning. Relax and let your music quiet your mind.

AT LEAST 15 MINUTES

Connect with Your Pets

***Benefits*:** Pets bring so much joy. They are known to reduce stress, lower blood pressure, and lessen your risk for depression. Spending time with animals will also lower your anxiety levels and give you a look into the mind-set of nonhuman animals, which is an act of mindfulness in itself.

How does cannabis help? Cannabis brings out those childlike qualities that lower inhibition and help you be in the present. Additionally, the heightened cognitive function that cannabis brings will allow you to actively engage with your pets in this mental self-care ritual.

HOW TO

1. Away from the company of your pets (no offense to them, we just don't want to get animals high as they can't consent) enjoy your favorite form of cannabis. Think about how much your animals mean to you and how, despite the joy they bring, you can get so busy that you forget to play with them! It's time to change that.
2. Once the marijuana starts to work its magic, approach your pets. Shake your arms and head a bit to get out of your mind and revel in the cannabis creeping up on you. All your worries and fears are taken care of. All you need to do right now is play with your pets.
3. Sit down with your pets. Watch them. Have they picked a nesting spot with a view of your door so that they can protect

you from any intruders? Do they seem overjoyed with an onset of attention from their human? Are they busy perfectly styling their hair? Have you noticed how absolutely adorable their paws are?

4. Engage them and play with them. Take a toy and toss it across your yard or roll it through your apartment. Watch your pets chase it down. Sprinkle some catnip on a scratcher and get a kick out of your cat having fun in its own elevated mind-set. Remind your dog what a good boy, the best boy, he is.
5. Enjoy the combination of the cannabis and playing with your pets. Notice how the herb relaxes your mind and makes you more social, agreeable, and playful.
6. Now, step away to consume more cannabis and reflect on what your pets taught you.

Throw Yourself a Dance Party

Benefits: Dancing is exercise. It strengthens your muscles and bones and encourages heart health. Emotionally, dancing can improve mood and fight stress, anxiety, and depression as endorphins and adrenaline spike during cardio workouts. All these benefits are amplified when your favorite song accompanies you as you kick up your heels.

How does cannabis help? Cannabis helps you quiet your mind and pay attention to how good it feels to move and stretch while connecting with your song of choice. Marijuana's effect on your senses makes music sound better and dancing feel more delightful. It also lowers your inhibitions, so you'll be more willing to get into your groove and dance like no one is watching!

HOW TO

1. Find an area big enough for you to comfortably dance. Sit down with your cannabis, phone, and headphones (or just your cannabis if you have speakers set up).
2. Indulge in magical Mary Jane. As you level up your consciousness, consider what musical selection you feel like grooving and moving to. From hip-hop to glam rock, reggae to metal, you can't go wrong if it makes you happy.
3. After you're adequately elevated, turn on your song or playlist, and dance like no one is watching. If you feel silly, lean into that goofiness with another hit of cannabis. Now is your time

to be free and totally yourself—just like a rock star. Don't take yourself too seriously.

4. Dance however you want, but really tap into the energy that your song of choice is putting out into the universe. Take another hit of cannabis as desired while the music plays. When the song is over, either keep dancing to the next or sit back down where you began.
5. Cannabis can not only enhance the senses but blur the lines between them. You may feel music in your body, or see colors radiate in coordination with the music and your dance moves.
6. Check in with your body. Release any tension; rub a cannabis topical into any places that ache. Cannabis is a pain reliever, both when applied topically and when inhaled or ingested.
7. Check in with your mind. How are things going in your head? Do you feel more motivated and powerful? How about confident and creative? Notice how the power of music, dance, and cannabis can change your entire state of mind.

THE DURATION OF A CONCERT

Experience a Concert

Benefits: Live music gives you the honor of seeing a band you love in person. You'll feel a sense of community through the other fans and will feel the stress melting away as you have fun.

How does cannabis help? Cannabis has a long-standing history of facilitating musical appreciation, which is why so many of your favorite rock stars smoke it. Edibles are particularly useful for attending concerts since the high that they provide lasts longer than the high from smoking. It's also a feel-good, full-body high, which makes dancing extra fun.

HOW TO

1. Check your local listings and buy concert tickets, making sure to invite any friends who will also appreciate the show. Spending money on concert tickets is never a purchase you regret.
2. The evening of, invite your friends over. Have snacks available—both for nourishment and for cannabis intake (your edibles). Consume the dose that works for you, and keep in mind that it can take up to an hour and a half for edibles' effects to be felt. If you consume an edible before a show, you don't have to worry about getting in trouble by bringing anything into the show (you don't want any paranoia ruining your good time).
3. Take public transit, call a cab, or have someone sober take you to the show. Then, when you get there, go wild and let loose. Notice how your awareness of sound is heightened, and see

how the songs make you feel. Are they invoking any memories or emotions? Are you noticing chord changes or messages in lyrics that went over your head previously? How is your vision enhanced? Are there beautiful visuals that go with the music? Do you notice how much fun the crowd is having? How does your body feel about totally letting go and dancing and singing along?

4. In addition to enhancing your senses, let the cannabis relax you. Everyone is only interested in having a good time. No one cares how sweaty you are, how your voice sounds, or what you look like when you dance. Use the power of Mary Jane to let go completely.
5. When the show ends, take a moment to soak in and appreciate the night. Now, it's time to plan the next concert.

AT LEAST 30 MINUTES

Catch Up On a TV Show

***Benefits*:** Watching TV is an easy and affordable way to give your brain a break from stress and help your mind decompress. It can also have educational benefits, depending on what you're in the mood to watch, and can provide comfort when you're feeling lonely.

How does cannabis help? Cannabis helps you expand your mind and enjoy the arts. The heightened senses and appreciation that cannabis brings can cause movies and TV to be more entertaining. The plant also reminds you that it's okay to slow down, relax, and rest every now and then.

HOW TO

1. Select the TV show that you would like to enjoy. Are you in the mood for a visually stimulating documentary, a comedy to laugh along with, or your favorite "guilty pleasure" TV show?
2. Grab the method of cannabis intake that you would like to enjoy and indulge in your herb.
3. Make sure delicious and healthy snacks are set out, then turn on the TV or your digital device and enjoy. Feel your stress drain away as you turn your focus toward the storyline of your show. If you're watching at night, ensure a good night's sleep by giving yourself about an hour of screen-free time just before bedtime.

Try a Metta Meditation

***Benefits*:** A loving-kindness meditation, also known as a metta meditation, will help you let go of your worries and bring in peace and appreciation, easing your transition from one activity to another (like work to home, or chasing the kids to quiet time with your partner) and leaving you feeling thankful for the rest of your day or evening.

How does cannabis help? Cannabis, in particular indicas or indica-dominant hybrids, is a stress killer. Adding cannabis to your meditation will help your brain relax and transition more easily into a new, calmer activity.

HOW TO

1. Once you're ready to move from a hectic activity to one that's more low-key, find somewhere quiet. This may be a corner at your office before you head out for happy hour, or back home before heading out for dinner plans.
2. Consume cannabis. If you are at the office, a few drops of cannabis tincture under your tongue may be the best method of intake. If you are somewhere safe to smoke or vaporize, spark up a relaxing indica. Get into lotus pose by sitting cross-legged and putting each foot on the opposite thigh. Feel the power of the plant work to de-stress your brain.
3. Choose a mantra—a word or phrase that carries significance and that you can repeat to harness the power of the words—to direct loving energy toward yourself and others. "May I be

happy" is commonly used, although you could also use "May I be calm," "May I be loved," "May I be strong," or a mantra of your choosing. Say the mantra out loud or in your head, depending on your surroundings.

4. Inhale and wish loving-kindness on yourself, chanting "May I be happy." Then exhale and blow out the stress, worries, and fears of the day.
5. Now pick a loved one and wish them loving-kindness. As you inhale, chant "May you be happy." Continue to exhale the day's stress.
6. Next, inhale and wish happiness on someone with whom you have a difficult relationship. Inhale and chant "May you be happy," then exhale your harsh thoughts.
7. Finally, inhale and wish the world loving-kindness, chanting "May the world be happy" (or whatever variation you are using). Repeat the rounds as desired.
8. Enjoy the rest of your day from a place of love.

AT LEAST 30 MINUTES

Enjoy Literature

Benefits: Reading books stimulates the mind, increases your vocabulary, and aids in analytical thinking. This self-care ritual allows you to take a break from the real world and teleport yourself into another one, letting you relax and de-stress.

How does cannabis help? Cannabis is a psychedelic that can expand your consciousness and imagination. You may find yourself giving characters silly voices and experiencing the setting coming alive in new ways while reading with cannabis.

HOW TO

1. Sit down somewhere comfy. Make sure you have your book, your cannabis, a cozy blanket, and a cup of tea or a glass of wine if you like. Be sure you have enough light to read by as well.
2. Light up as you begin reading. Let the characters and plot come alive. What does this other world look like? Imagine yourself dropping right into the book, into the imaginary world, and watch the events unfold. What do you see, hear, smell, touch, and even taste?
3. Focus your state of mind on staying present in the universe of your book and have as much fun while you're there as possible. Allow this cannabis self-care ritual to relax and expand your mind as you travel through this new world.

Write a Love Letter

Benefits: Writing helps you express, process, and release emotions. Writing a letter not only makes the person the message is addressed to feel more cared for, but you yourself will feel more cared for as you reflect on how much someone means to you.

How does cannabis help? Cannabis facilitates creativity, and writing the letter becomes more natural with a lifted mind. It also can healthily lower inhibitions, so you'll feel more comfortable sharing emotions. Cannabis just makes you feel good all around, and when you feel good, you're more likely to want to share your joy.

HOW TO

1. Sit somewhere calm, with a pen, paper, and cannabis. Feel free to use your computer if you want, but don't be afraid to use this opportunity to unplug and express your emotions away from distracting electronics.
2. Stay seated for however long feels right while partaking in cannabis. As you become higher and your mind expands, ask yourself, who needs more love in their life? Is there anyone who you have been extra appreciative of lately? Decide who to dedicate your love letter to. It can be a romantic partner, a friend, a family member, a celebrity you admire, or even yourself. Love letters do not exclusively belong to romantic relationships.

3. Begin writing. Don't worry about grammar or sentence structure. Focus on why you love this person, and using that as a muse, express yourself and your emotions.
4. Inhale cannabis as you please during the writing process, but especially when you find yourself unsure what to say next. When writer's block hits, sit back, inhale cannabis, and simply think about the happiness this person gives you. You'll be smiling and writing in no time.
5. When you're finished writing the letter, reward yourself for adding love to the world with a hit of cannabis.
6. What happens next is up to you. You can go ahead and give your loved one the letter and experience the joy of watching them know how cherished they are. Or you can let it sit and revisit it another time before deciding whether to send it or not. Either way, notice how much better you feel having processed and released your emotions in such a loving manner.

AT LEAST 10 MINUTES

Wake Up with CBD Coffee

Benefits: There are benefits to pausing between waking up and starting your day; you'll have lower stress levels and be more productive in the long run. Coffee enhances brain function and physical skills, and even helps protect you from dementia and Parkinson's disease.

How does cannabis help? Do you ever wake up feeling anxious? CBD helps with that. It also reduces pain, which is great if you're feeling stiff in the morning. It pairs perfectly with coffee to ease you into a productive day.

HOW TO

1. When you wake up, after turning off the alarm, don't check your email. Instead, head into the kitchen, noticing the sunlight, and brew a cup of coffee.
2. When it's ready, take your cup of coffee and CBD into a sunlit area of your home. Morning light helps the body wake up.
3. If you are using a CBD tincture, drop some directly into your coffee. If you have a CBD vape, feel fancy by taking hits between sips.
4. For the time it takes to finish the cup, sit in silence. Stay away from electronics. Savor each rich, earthy sip. Notice how your brain and body gradually come awake to meet the day.

Visit a Cannabis Farm

Benefits: Admiring the plants standing proud in all their glory, and learning about the effort that goes into keeping these plants happy, offers a newfound understanding and appreciation for cannabis.

How does cannabis help? You are able to more deeply connect with and respect the plant while enjoying it. Cannabis treats stress, anxiety disorders, and depression, so let it usher away bad vibes so you can experience your cannabis trip fully.

HOW TO

1. Do some research and pick a cannabis farm to visit that best fits your needs and budget. A simple Google search for "cannabis farm tours" will bring up a plethora of results, or, if you have a brand that you adore, find which growers they buy cannabis from and then visit those farms. That way, you can see the plants you use up close in person.
2. Make arrangements for the trip. Invite friends along who will also appreciate the tour and arrange safe travel back and forth so you can indulge in cannabis without worry.
3. By yourself or with your friends, partake in cannabis. If possible smoke a joint so you can touch and observe the buds of the plant.
4. When you arrive at the cannabis farm, let your tour guide lead you. Relax, observe, and listen. Admire the plants. If you're at an outdoor farm, see how tall they stretch to meet the sun

that feeds them. If you're at an indoor farm, notice the meticulous care that the growers provide by hand to keep the plants happy.

5. Utilize your heightened senses. How do the leaves look? What shade of green are they? Inspect their beautiful buds. Do you notice other colors, such as purple and orange? Do your buds at home feel more sacred now that you see the entire plant? How do they smell? Observe the natural magnificence of the plants and take your newfound respect home with you.

Go Out with Friends

Benefits: Studies show that people with friends are healthier, both physically and mentally. A support system is crucial during hard times, and happy times become better with a group of friends you love. Foster that with a night out.

How does cannabis help? Sharing cannabis between friends is shown to strengthen bonds. Cannabis is also a fun alcohol substitute if you want to stay out and have fun but don't want to risk a hangover the next day.

HOW TO

1. Meet your friends at someone's home. Put on music, catch up, and pass around some cannabis.
2. While you're all connected, high, and relaxed, decide what the plan is. Dancing? Karaoke? Safely head out.
3. Allow the marijuana to help you cut loose. Go out on the dance floor and sing along to the music as loud as you like.
4. Cheer on your friends. If you notice them having a good time, grooving out, flirting, or telling terrific jokes, make sure to let them know how much you appreciate them.

AT LEAST 20 MINUTES

Call an Old Friend

***Benefits*:** Catching up with an old friend will help you feel heard and understood. Your friend will share appreciation for what's happened in your life as you share pride for what's happened in theirs. Additionally, connecting with someone you haven't caught up with in a while not only removes any guilt but will bring you joy as you reconnect.

How does cannabis help? Cannabis boosts confidence, giving you the nudge to go ahead and press the call button. It also lowers social anxiety and will get you through any feelings of awkwardness. Consuming the plant makes you a mindful listener and will help you tune in to what your friend has to share.

HOW TO

1. Grab your phone and find somewhere quiet and safe. Indulge in cannabis. As you consume, reflect on this person and all the good times you've had together. Let your heart fill with love for them. Make a mental checklist of all their attributes you admire and the times that they gave your life joy.
2. Reflect on all that has occurred since you two have hung out or had a proper catch-up. Forgive yourself for letting time slip by, and allow your mind to open up with all the possibilities of what your friend may have experienced since you last spoke.
3. Once you feel settled, pick up your phone and give them a call.
4. Let your friend talk first. Practice listening. Using the patient properties of cannabis, sincerely let them know you hold love

and happiness for their journey. Offer honest advice if they ask for it.

5. When it's your turn to talk about your life, open your mind and heart, share what's changed, fill them in on your joy and your pains.
6. Keep a receptive mind and listen to their thoughts and advice. Welcome their perspective.
7. When it's time to go, let them know how much they mean to you. Remember that people can remain friends even through the passage of time and distance, and let yourself off the hook for allowing so much time to pass. Focus on the knowledge that you have a friendship that can survive distance and time, and give gratitude for that.

10 MINUTES

Release Your Paranoia

Benefits: Releasing paranoia through meditation and breath work lets you exhale anxieties and unhelpful, intrusive thoughts and become grounded and calm.

How does cannabis help? CBD fights paranoia and counteracts the sometimes uncomfortable psychoactive effects that can accompany high-THC strains if you take too much. Adding CBD to meditation and deep breathing gives these stress-busting tools an extra source of power.

HOW TO

1. Begin by identifying what's making you paranoid. Maybe it's an intrusive thought? Maybe you saw something concerning? Or maybe you took too much of a certain strain that doesn't sit right with you.
2. Remove yourself from your current setting and find a new quiet spot to sit with your CBD.
3. Close your eyes and imagine yourself inside a vast forest. It's quiet except for the noise of friendly animals. You feel naturally safe.
4. Begin taking deep breaths. Visualize yourself exhaling all your paranoia in the form of dark, grey strands that form a cloud of worry in the center of the forest clearing.
5. Visualize Goddess Mary Jane emerging from the forest. Let your mind create the version meant for you. She approaches you and hands you CBD from a bag she is carrying.

6. Whether it's a tincture, vape, or edible, accept the gift from Mary Jane and consume the CBD. Return to your breath work.
7. As you exhale, imagine your breath blowing away all the paranoia. Mary Jane helps and uses her superpowers to open up the tree tops.
8. When you're ready to leave the forest, open your eyes. Know that Mary Jane is taking care of you. You can consume as much CBD as you need. When you're ready, head back with a calmer state of mind, knowing this plant is here to keep you safe.

AT LEAST 30 MINUTES

Remind Yourself of Your Self-Worth

Benefits: The rhythmic chanting of mantras provides stress relief. The practice is also known to decrease fear and worrisome thoughts, increasing positivity and self-esteem.

How does cannabis help? Research shows that using cannabis, and therefore activating the cannabinoid system, reduces stress-related anxiety. THC is similar to anandamide, a neurotransmitter produced naturally in the brain known as the "bliss molecule." With lowered stress, the mind can more easily enter a meditative state conducive to manifesting higher self-esteem.

HOW TO

1. Sit down and consume cannabis, then begin free journaling by writing about how you feel and what you want to change in your life. Consider what you wish to manifest. Are you ready to ask for a raise? Do you want to take your relationship to the next level? Do you want to feel more confident and powerful in general?
2. Once you've identified your desire turn it into a single affirming and declarative sentence. This may involve surrendering to the universe, such as, "I feel good. I trust the process of life." Or your mantra could be more specific, such as "I am magnificent; I am loved" or "I am powerful; I deserve abundance."
3. Move to a space where you can meditate in peace. Bring your cannabis and your mantra. Begin inhaling and exhaling,

adding the inhalation of cannabis to your breath work to help you sink into your body and retain focus.

4. Inhale and say your mantra. Out loud is better as you get the added benefits of chanting, which decreases stress and aids in positive thinking. When you exhale, imagine all your self-doubt or fears exiting your body with your breath. Continue this practice for as long as you can.
5. With time, the mantra you created as part of this mental self-care ritual will become part of you. As this happens, it will also come true.

Take a Mental Health Day

Benefits: Mental health days give your brain time to rest and reboot. They'll help you become more productive in the long-run by preventing stress and exhaustion from building up to a detrimental level.

How does cannabis help? In addition to treating stress itself, marijuana addresses stress-related conditions, such as migraines, and physical pain and stiffness related to work and lifestyle issues (sitting hunched over a computer all day, for instance). It's also been shown to work as a sleep aid, so it can help you rest on your mental health day.

HOW TO

1. Begin planning and assessing the best way for you to take a mental health day. After all, if you're already experiencing burnout, it is not a lie to tell your boss or partner that you need a sick day.
2. Your mental health day is for you. Sleep in. If you need help taking a nap or falling asleep, try a heavy indica. With the aid of cannabis, give yourself permission to turn off your brain. Rest, watch TV, read a book, and snuggle with your pets.
3. Or if your version of a mental health day includes finally tackling your chores or to-do list, use an invigorating sativa strain.
4. Throughout the day, check in with your body. Treat physical pain and stiffness with a cannabis topical. If you're experiencing digestive issues, marijuana is also known to provide nausea

relief. Remember, a body that feels good can help your mind reboot.

5. Return to your regular schedule feeling rested and rebooted. Remember to work in as many regular mental health days as you can to function as healthily and happily as possible.

15 MINUTES

Increase Your Creativity with Alternate Nostril Breathing

***Benefits*:** Alternate nostril breathing, an invigorating form of breath work, is known to boost energy. Using it as part of this self-care exercise will help you get rid of creative blocks and bring in new ideas.

How does cannabis help? Cannabis consumption becomes a form of meditative breathing when you intentionally inhale deeply and exhale slowly. Cannabis opens the mind as a psychedelic and stimulates the imagination to generate new ideas. Meditative breathing with cannabis unlocks creative doors.

HOW TO

1. Step away from the creative project you are working on and sit in a quiet place on a pillow or blanket. Bring cannabis in a smokable or vaporizable form with you, along with a notepad and a pen.
2. Take a hit of cannabis. Slowly and deeply inhale it. Feel the herb stimulate your mind and open your lungs. Then slowly and intentionally exhale the smoke.
3. When you're at a comfortable high, begin alternate nostril breathing: Place your hands, open to receive, on your knees. Then hold your right thumb against the right nostril to close it and inhale deeply through your left nostril. Pinch closed your left nostril with your ring finger, release your thumb from the

right nostril, and exhale through your right nostril. Then inhale through the right nostril, cover that nostril, and unclose the left nostril and exhale through the left. Inhale then through the left nostril, cover that nostril, and exhale through the right. Continue this breath work for 10 minutes.

4. During this period, allow your mind to go blank by letting worrisome or distracting thoughts come and go like leaves blowing in the wind. Whenever your creative project pops up, say hello and then let it pass.
5. As the cannabis takes effect in combination with the invigorating alternate nostril breathing, you will notice your meditation begins to change. First, you will experience calmness. Then, watch how fresh ideas bubble up and come to you. Begin to jot down inspiration with your nearby pen and paper.
6. When you're ready, fully open your eyes. Stretch a bit and notice your calm yet creative state of mind. Take your time and then return to your creative work with a fresh mind and new ideas.

15 MINUTES

Tap Into Positive Thinking

Benefits: Studies show that positive thinking produces better stress-coping skills and lowers depression rates. It also raises confidence and self-love, which can unlock a world of opportunities.

How does cannabis help? Cannabis aids in divergent thinking, which is the mind's ability to explore multiple solutions to a problem. Such mind expansion will help you turn pessimism into optimism by considering the best outcome rather than the worst. Humor also aids in positive thinking, and cannabis is perfect for creating laughter.

HOW TO

1. Grab your cannabis and sit on the floor or in your favorite chair.
2. Take a few moments to breathe mindfully with cannabis. Deeply inhale the herb, and then exhale all the way. Repeat several rounds until your mind is happily elevated.
3. Continue to deeply inhale and exhale, but don't stress about counts. What is on your mind? Are you convinced a romance is doomed? Perhaps you are catastrophizing about something that happened at work. Or maybe you simply want to break thought patterns that no longer serve you.
4. We base much of negative thinking upon the idea that the worst-case scenario will come true. For a second, consider

what would happen if the opposite were true? Imagine living a life in which the best possible scenario comes true.

5. Black-and-white thinking is another thing that produces negative thoughts. Now, work on considering the middle ground, the grey area of all the possibilities rather than the extremes. For example, do you tend to take things personally? What if your boss's email wasn't personal, but they were simply stressed? Remind yourself how we all struggle and how it's unhelpful to assume everything is an attack on you.
6. Consume more cannabis if needed, and then ask yourself: Is there any humor in the situation that has you down? Tap into your sense of humor and allow yourself to laugh if you can.
7. Finally, conclude the thought work and meditation. Call a friend you trust who is good at seeing the best in the world. Share what's on your mind and complete the exercise by getting some healthy outside perspective. Work on integrating these new ways of thinking into your everyday life.

2–4 HOURS

Decorate Your Lighters

Benefits: Decorating your lighters combines the healing stress relief of an art project with a useful final product. It can also help you become a better decision-maker by sharpening cognitive function while increasing creativity and innovative thinking.

How does cannabis help? Cannabis encourages creativity by helping your brain scan through a myriad of solutions, which you can then turn into an original craft project. It keeps your energy levels up and your mind focused as you create.

HOW TO

1. To begin, consider how many lighters have gone missing since you started using cannabis. Then imagine what your dream lighter would look like. Is it covered in puffy paint and glitter? Is your name on it? Is it decorated with stickers and goofy googly eyes?
2. Buy your supplies. You can find craft supplies and bulk packages of lighters online or at your local craft store.
3. Partake in cannabis and then go wild. Glue pom-poms and sequins onto pink lighters. Use puff paint to draw the name of your favorite band on a black lighter. Turn a green lighter into a magical marijuana-themed lighter by adding purple and orange glitter.
4. Let the lighters dry. When they're ready, celebrate this mental self-care activity by trying out one of your craft projects and lighting up some herb.

15 MINUTES

Try a Clarity Meditation

Benefits: Studies show that uncertainty is more stressful than bad news. Whether it's deciding what the next career move should be or figuring out how to make up with a friend, clarity brings you mental peace and a road map to move forward.

How does cannabis help? Cannabis helps you obtain mental clarity by raising dopamine, a brain chemical known to aid in focus. By integrating cannabis into this meditation you transform uncertainty into a clear path forward.

HOW TO

1. Grab something comfy to sit on and cannabis.
2. Inhale for one count, exhale for one count. Inhale a hit of cannabis for one, exhale the smoke or vapor for one. Repeat until you're in a heightened state of your personal comfort.
3. Set down the cannabis and continue to breathe. Allow the stressful situation to marinate in your mind. Do not fear uncomfortable feelings.
4. Thoughts and feelings will naturally arise. Embrace them and let them inform your thought process. For example, you may decide that your love for your partner outweighs whatever they did to upset you and let it go. Perhaps a friendship ran its course and it's time to put up boundaries.
5. Once you've found clarity, open your eyes. Notice how much better it feels to have reached a decision and to have practiced mental self-care. Intentionally act on what you uncovered.

AN HOUR (THIS IS A PROJECT YOU CAN RETURN TO PERIODICALLY)

Plan Your Dream Vacation

***Benefits*:** Walking through the steps of planning a vacation creates the road map that kicks off the trip, turning it from a dream vacation to a real one. Just because you can't take your dream vacation right now doesn't mean it will never happen. Planning leads to manifestation through sparking hope and excitement, which encourage action. There's a very well-organized vacation ahead of you.

How does cannabis help? Studies show that cannabis can help you get work done (without the crash of stimulants). Marijuana also stimulates the frontal lobe of the brain, which is useful in creative projects, and helps turn close-minded thinking such as "I can never afford this" into problem-solving thinking such as "I can find a way."

HOW TO

1. Find a spot where you are at your most productive (be it your at-home desk or the couch in your living room), then consume cannabis. Let your ideal destination arise. You may have a place already in mind, or you may need to close your eyes and visualize as your mind expands.
2. Once you've settled on a place, begin researching either online or in a travel book. On your social media, put a call out for people who have already traveled there. What can you learn from them?

3. Figure out a budget. If the trip isn't something you can afford now, set up monthly bank transfers, and look to see what costs you can divert toward the trip. Look into travel hacks, such as setting up an email airfare price alert to ensure you don't overspend. Compare the cost of a hotel versus renting a room.
4. Don't forget the details, such as checking passport requirements and local cannabis laws, and ensure there isn't a season to avoid (such as hurricane season in the Caribbean). Check off all your to-do boxes.
5. Hang up a photo of the destination in your home or office. A visual reminder will keep you motivated by filling you with excitement.
6. Once your adventure becomes a reality, go forth and enjoy. Use your mindfulness skills to be present for your trip that you worked so hard for.

AN HOUR

Start a Scrapbook

Benefits: Creating a scrapbook can help you emotionally process your previous experiences. Your old photos can provide support as you grieve the past, and the blank pages ahead can remind you that you have a future.

How does cannabis help? Cannabis helps break you out of old ways of thinking. It's been shown to aid in emotional processing by reducing negative bias. Scrapbooking with cannabis will not only mean a cooler-looking scrapbook, but having this medicine by your side will help you cope with any difficult emotions that may arise.

HOW TO

1. First collect your supplies. All you need to start a scrapbook is a blank notebook, glue or tape, embellishments of your choosing, and items such as photos, postcards, and other memorabilia that you keep in a dusty box somewhere.
2. Sit down on the floor with your supplies and cannabis somewhere you can get messy. Cover the floor with old newspaper if needed.
3. Smoke up. Enjoy the inhalation of cannabis smoke or vapor as you envision the scrapbook coming to life. Watch the photos and mementos dance around in your mind as you mentally begin organizing.
4. Next, get messy. Paste photos, create borders out of colored paper, throw a sticker on there. Write dates and notes in the

corner. It doesn't have to look perfect; it only has to give you satisfaction and honor your life in a way that you relate to. Continue to consume cannabis as needed. Craft away for as long as you like.

5. Sit back, enjoy cannabis, and admire your work as the glue dries. It's okay to get emotional about all the people you've met and places you've been, while noting the many pages to follow and envisioning all that is to come. Remember that scrapbooking is a treasured craft because it helps us mourn, remember, and honor all that we've experienced.
6. Keep your scrapbook somewhere safe, and add to it as life unfolds. If you like, share it with someone you care about.

Enjoy Creative Collaboration

Benefits: Spending time with friends lifts self-esteem and provides a sense of belonging while reducing stress and depression levels. Studies show that people with close friends are happier and cope better with trauma due to the community friends provide. Creative collaboration leads to a better project as two (or more) heads are better than one.

How does cannabis help? Cannabis enhances creativity and is especially useful when shared within a group. Cannabis also helps with patience, opens your mind to proposals made by others, and decreases conflict.

HOW TO

1. The next time you're with your group of friends, pass around cannabis and begin brainstorming. Chances are there is a creative group project that you've already discussed, such as playing music, putting together a regular event, starting a podcast, or creating an online blog or zine. Decide what is best for your friend group and begin planning. Split up the jobs among yourselves by skill, interest, and availability.
2. Now that you have a plan, focus on the commitment. Whether it's weekly, biweekly, or monthly, commit to getting together to work on this project, on a schedule that is doable for everyone. Once you have a schedule in place remember to honor that commitment.

3. When you are together during this sacred creative time, remember to have fun (cannabis can help this). Make your work shine, but prioritize your love for your friends above your creative endeavors. Be kind. Make jokes. Laugh. Listen to one another. Let others speak. Consider criticism as an effort to improve the project rather than a personal attack. Make a pact that your relationships with one another come first.
4. With that in mind, let your dreams come true and be the rock star you always yearned to be. Get as goofy as you want on your podcast; cover the topics you see missing from other publications in your blog or zine. Watch with pride as you see the creative fruits of a group of friends come alive. Your finished product is the offspring of the combined minds of your group and the self-care that you prioritized to make it happen, as well as a beautiful reflection of your friendships.

Keep a Cannabis Journal

Benefits: Various cannabis strains and methods of intake produce different effects. And everyone reacts differently, so your experience with one strain may be different than a friend's. Maintaining a record helps you identify your favorite strains, the best ones for different settings, and how your tolerance evolves. This knowledge protects your mind from negative cannabis experiences such as paranoia and helps you learn about marijuana through journaling.

How does cannabis help? The heightened cognitive function that cannabis brings will help you articulate how different strains, methods of delivery, and dosage affect you.

HOW TO

1. Purchase a blank journal. Create a page for each entry that simply notes the date, which strain you used, where you got the strain from (as even cannabis with the same name can vary in effect depending on how and where it's grown), how much cannabis you consumed, the method of intake, and what your experience was like. It's also worth noting the setting.
2. Practice self-care by enjoying a cannabis experience. Eat an edible and go to a concert, enjoy a joint while catching up with a friend, or puff a vape while watching a movie.
3. Before the high and the memory of the experience fades away, jot down what happened. Did you feel a little underwhelmed, as if your edible tolerance has gone up and you wish you'd

eaten another half of a gummy before the show? Did the joint make you feel anxious, and is it a strain you want to avoid in the future? Did your vape cartridge make you laugh harder than you ever have, and you must stock up on more? Write down everything that comes to mind in the page next to the specific data info.

4. Continue to use your journal after each elevated experience. Use it to keep track of your tolerance and your favorite strains and ones to avoid. Going forward, this knowledge will help you curate an ideal cannabis-influenced self-care practice.

15 MINUTES

Try Aromatherapy

***Benefits*:** Various essential oils have different benefits, and inhaling essential oils is a safe way to produce a myriad of mental effects, from boosting motivation to anxiety relief. For example, lavender oil is relaxing. Lemon is uplifting. Sage calms and protects. Eucalyptus wakes you up. Cinnamon is spicy and stimulating.

How does cannabis help? Cannabis and essential oils both contain terpenes, or oils responsible for each plant's unique smell and flavor profile. Depending on which cannabis strain you use, the terpenes can be uplifting and floral, invigorating and citrus-flavored, or relaxing with earthy notes. Understanding how various strains affect us is an ongoing science, but currently indicas are associated with calm body highs, while sativas are associated with uplifting cerebral effects. Coupling cannabis, which enhances the senses, with other scents packs a double punch of homeopathic medicine.

HOW TO

1. Decide what mood adjustment you need and gather the necessary supplies. Consider having a variety of cannabis strains, from a motivating Lemon Haze to a calming Northern Lights, on hand. Life is not consistent. Some days we need calm and on others we need stimulation. This requires taking different forms of plant medicine depending on the situation. The same principle works for essential oils. The invigorating

eucalyptus can be helpful on a day for cleaning while rose oil may relax you after a date, so consider building a collection.

2. Seat yourself on a pillow or yoga mat somewhere sacred to you. Keep your cannabis and essential oil nearby. How can plant medicine—cannabis and the many others made into essential oils—best serve you right now?
3. Deeply inhale your relaxing lavender, zesty lemon, or cleansing sage and feel the effects spread through your body. Notice how your mind opens up and how powerful your sense of smell truly is. More than any other sense, smell is linked to memory. What does the scent remind you of?
4. Take a puff of your joint or a hit of your vape pen. How does the taste and smell of the cannabis pair with your essential oil or herb? Can you feel the earth notes, the citrus flavor, or the chilled-out floral flavor in your cannabis? Cannabis enhances the senses so may amplify your aromatherapeutic experience.
5. Repeat as desired. Notice how the cannabis and aromatherapy complement one another and take it all in as you engage in this mental self-care ritual.

AT LEAST 30 MINUTES

Organize Your Cannabis Supplies

Benefits: Organizing your cannabis is a ritual that puts you in touch with both your herb and your needs while creating a valuable outcome—a tidy stash that's both visually appealing and easy to use. Organization reduces stress and provides a healthier environment for both you and your bud.

How does cannabis help? Research shows that marijuana can stimulate dopamine, a neurotransmitter that can regulate your emotional responses. Cannabis can also help you stay on task as you organize your flower, without any jitters or comedown.

HOW TO

1. Sit down with your cannabis and a pen and paper and make a plan. As you enjoy your flower, figure out what makes sense given your living arrangements. Cannabis buds should be kept in airtight containers away from direct light, heat, and humidity. Are you interested in keeping your cannabis on display? If so, mason jars or glass containers available at a homewares store or head shop are most visually pleasing. If you need to keep your cannabis out of sight, wooden or opaque glass containers work best. The best storage unit for cannabis concentrates is smaller (about the size of a quarter) containers. Edibles can be stored in your fridge or freezer (but don't forget to mark them!), and tinctures last a long time happy in their tincture bottles.

2. Pick up your supplies either online or in person to fit your needs. Keep in mind you want to separate flower by strain, and you will also need a storage container for all your cannabis accessories. Lighters, smoking devices, edibles, and other cannabis accessories should be kept separate from your flower. You don't want your cannabis picking up any outside odors.
3. Organize any cannabis flower by strain. Use stickers or a label maker to mark each by name and type (indica, hybrid, or sativa).
4. Next organize your smoking devices, lighters, ashtrays, and other accessories somewhere nearby for easy access but not mixed with your flowers. Keep them on display if you like, or if you need to be discreet, cushioned stash bags are readily available online.
5. Whether it's on a shelf (away from direct sunlight!) or tucked under your bed, find a safe and secure area to keep your cannabis. Now that it's well-organized and accessible, using it becomes that much easier, decluttering your mind as well as your environment.

PART 3

Spirit

Create Art for Self-Acceptance

Benefits: Creating art aids in personal growth, self-esteem, and self-acceptance and studies show that art therapy can help the brain process and move past difficult or traumatic events.

How does cannabis help? Research has demonstrated that cannabis helps fight the effects of difficult or traumatic events that can lead to self-doubt. The plant is also a stress and anxiety killer, which will help you take the edge off and make it easier for you to accept yourself...flaws and all.

HOW TO

1. Pick up your art supplies of choice. Set up a space where you can enjoy cannabis and create art in peace.
2. After consuming some cannabis, begin the difficult task of examining why you feel down. Realize that difficult emotions and past pain may arise. When this happens, take a hit of cannabis to comfort you. Utilize your art supplies to turn your feelings into art. Art doesn't have to be pretty or perfect. No one needs to see this but you. Your art can be scary, messy, and imperfect. The goal is to get your self-doubt out of you and onto the paper to help you process it, not to create something fit for a museum.
3. When you feel finished with what you've created, step back and observe. What do you see? How does it make you feel? Consume cannabis as you look at your art to calm any lingering anxiety or stress.

4. Consuming more cannabis as needed, reflect inward again. What does life look like when you are your most authentic self? Are you in a relationship? Independent? Enjoying career success? Traveling?
5. As you visualize, put pen to paper again and draw (or paint, etc.) what comes to mind. Do not hold back in creating an image of all that you want and deserve.
6. When you finish, observe this second piece. Know that your vision is achievable, and you are worthy of it regardless of what gives you self-doubt.

30 MINUTES

Go Flower Shopping

Benefits: Nurturing your soul by spending time around flowers can reduce stress and anxiety and has also been shown to improve brain function and encourage creativity.

How does cannabis help? Cannabis heightens senses to make you more in touch with the flowers' colors and smells, which can lift your mood, lighten your spirit, and affect your power of recall, bringing joyful memories to mind.

HOW TO

1. Consume cannabis at home. Consider trying an edible as it lasts a long time and you don't have to travel with it. Walk around your living space. What could you use a dash of? Happiness and sunshine? Romantic love? Exotic beauty? Calm serenity?
2. As the cannabis starts to kick in, either walk or have someone you trust drive you to the local florist.
3. Look around at all the beauty. Use your elevated senses to enjoy what you see. Imagine that you are entering a sacred, secret garden.
4. Stop and smell the flowers. How does the scent of roses make you feel? What about lilies, or lilacs? Enjoy aromatherapy from real plants and notice what speaks to you.
5. Take as much time as you need to peruse through the store. Consider the energy that you want to bring into your home. For example, roses can act as an aphrodisiac in the bedroom

or simply make you feel loved. A vase of sunflowers in the kitchen invokes a smile. The magnificent bird-of-paradise is sure to solicit a feeling of awe. Orchids are associated with the feminine and beauty. When you've found what feels right, head to the register and check out. Once you're back home, carefully and meditatively place the flowers around your home to honor the plants and remember the spiritual self-care journey they took you on.

10 MINUTES

Practice the Fourfold Flower Power Breath

Benefits: This fourfold breath is a form of pranayama, the practice of controlling your breath to help relax your body, mind, and spirit. This spiritual self-care activity calms your nerves, eases anxiety, and reduces stress. This breathing technique is also celebrated for its grounding properties. Use it to find balance when you're feeling overwhelmed.

How does cannabis help? CBD helps calm your nerves and settle into the breath work. Especially when consumed while already in a meditative state, cannabis can help you more fully inhabit your body, so you feel every inhale and exhale and stay in the moment. Opt for a high-CBD strain for this grounding exercise.

HOW TO

1. Set up a pillow or yoga mat where you can sit quietly. Place a glass of water and your cannabis within arm's reach.
2. Set a timer for 8 minutes. In numerology and some pagan practices, the number 8 represents balance—an eternity symbol flipped on its side. Or if you dislike the sound of timers and alarms, conduct this self-care ritual at a pace and length that feels right for you.
3. Inhale for four counts and hold the breath for four counts. Exhale for four counts and hold for four counts. Repeat.

Count at your own pace, but don't rush it. Settle into your body. Relax. Take your time.

4. After several rounds of the fourfold breath, integrate cannabis into your breath work. Inhale the calming CBD for four breaths and hold for four breaths. Slowly exhale the smoke or vapor for four counts. Hold for four counts. Repeat as desired. Rather than spending continuous rounds using cannabis, integrate it as desired. Continuous inhalation may lead to coughing. It's okay if this occurs; have a sip of water, and then return to the exercise.
5. As you enter a grounded state of calm you will begin to feel more grounded in your body. Notice what arises. Is there stiffness in your neck you weren't aware of? Tightness in your shoulders and chest from stress? Make a mental note of what you discover the deeper you sink into the breath work.
6. Continue the fourfold breath and the cannabis/CBD integration until your timer goes off and 8 minutes have passed, or until your body says it's ready.
7. Before getting up and returning to your daily activities, take a moment to address anything that arose in your body. Stretch, do some neck rolls, or massage knots of tension.

20 MINUTES

Try a Nighttime Meditation for Sleep

Benefits: Studies have shown that meditating before sleep drastically reduces insomnia. Sleep deprivation reeks havoc on our emotional selves, making it difficult to tap into our spiritual side. A good night's sleep also allows us to enter the dream world, which always has lessons to teach us.

How does cannabis help? The phytocannabinoids in cannabis attach to your endogenous cannabinoid system and help create a calm state of mind conducive for meditation. Research shows that phytocannabinoids such as THC enable you to fall asleep, stay asleep, experience deeper sleep, and even breathe better while sleeping. If you know which strain is sedating for you, trust your body. When in doubt, opt for a heavy indica for deep sleep.

HOW TO

1. After you've finished getting ready for bed, sit meditatively in your bedroom and practice deep cannabis breathing. Inhale cannabis; exhale cannabis. Repeat for several rounds until you reach a state of mind comfortable to you.
2. Moving very slowly, lift yourself out of your seated position and into your bed. Tuck yourself in comfortably until you feel snug, safe, and ready for sleep.
3. Lie on your back. Focus your attention on your toes. Wiggle them. Inhale and stretch your toes widely. Then feel them becoming very heavy.

4. Let your toes relax as the heaviness spreads down your feet with an exhale. Thank your feet for carrying you around all day long. Move up to your calves. Again, flex and squeeze to remove any tension picked up during the day. Then let your calves rest heavily on your bed. Your bed frame and floor are sturdily supporting you.
5. Continue to move up your body, through your thighs, butt, belly and back, chest, and neck. For each area, flex to release tension with an inhale, and exhale as you sink into your mattress.
6. When you reach your head, notice the weight of your beautiful brain. It deserves a peaceful night in dreamland. Let the relaxing, safe cannabis and meditation carry you away as your entire body settles into your comfy sleep nest.
7. Imagine yourself floating on a beautiful, giant lily pad. You're safer than you've ever been in this magical place. You're floating down a dark blue river that matches the star-filled sky above. Nothing can hurt you here, in this land of spiritual self-care. Your only job is to surrender.

AT LEAST 15 MINUTES

Make an Unknown Pleasures List

Benefits: An unknown pleasures list enumerates goals that would be expansive to you personally. It's a bucket list for the soul. Creating one inspires you to take action to make the listed experiences happen, and reminds you of all you can look forward to in the future. It also emphasizes the importance of fun.

How does cannabis help? Research shows that cannabis increases hyper-priming, the brain's ability to form connections between seemingly unrelated concepts. Such thinking encourages expansive creativity. For instance, writing the name of a country you want to visit can rapidly trigger three other goals that might at first seem unrelated but that are in fact actions that advance you further toward your ultimate goal.

HOW TO

1. Sit somewhere comfortable with your cannabis and a pen and paper. At the top of your page of paper write "Unknown Pleasures."
2. Take a few minutes to indulge in cannabis, using your delivery method of choice. Move slowly. Feel the cannabis expand your mind and open it into a state of creative relaxation.
3. Let the brainstorming and soul searching begin. What adventures do you want to go on in this lifetime? What experiences will be expansive to you personally? What do you want to see? What do you want to achieve? What is the most fun you can imagine having? Start writing things down. List things that

give you joy simply by thinking about them. You can put career goals that will bring you great satisfaction but try to think outside of intents that are part of your regular schedule. This can include countries you want to visit, animals you want to see in the wild, skill sets you wish to learn, and whatever your heart desires.

4. When you run out of ideas, remind yourself that you can always add to this list. It is ever evolving, as are you.
5. Notice how you feel. Listing goals gives you motivation to manifest them. Writing down a martial art you yearn to master or a country you long to visit is the first step to making that dream come true.
6. Hang up your unknown pleasures list somewhere you'll see it on a regular basis, such as on a bulletin board in your home office or on your fridge. This will keep your eyes on the prize.
7. When you complete an unknown pleasure, check it off the list. Afterward, take a moment to say a prayer of gratitude for your ability to manifest dreams into reality.

20 MINUTES

Create an Email Chain for Gratitude

Benefits: Writing out what you're grateful for increases your mental strength, self-esteem, optimism, empathy, and physical health. It also helps you sleep more soundly and form connections with others. Creating a group gratitude email chain strengthens bonds between friends.

How does cannabis help? Cannabis contains mood-stabilizing properties that will help you notice the good in your life. The plant can also act as a focus tool to aid in writing. Try a creative hybrid such as Gelato, Headband, Blue Dream, or Girl Scout Cookies.

HOW TO

1. Sit down in front of your computer. Inhale cannabis to lift your spirits and help you focus.
2. In an email, create a list of everything you are grateful for. Your items can be as small as the spices in your pantry, or as grand as the fact that you are alive. Notice how typing out what you're grateful for creates a perspective shift.
3. When you finish your list, email it to friends who will appreciate a gratitude chain. The instructions, which you can add to the top of the email, are simple: "Write out what you're grateful for and pass it forward."
4. As the email chain grows, notice how reading others' lists reminds you of more things you're grateful for in your life.

AN HOUR

Get Rid of Things That Make You Angry

Benefits: You may not think of it this way, but cleaning out your home is exercise that raises your endorphins and makes you feel happy. Additionally, if you're harboring anger toward someone, getting rid of their things as a form of self-care removes reminders of them and opens the door to forgiveness.

How does cannabis help? Cannabis's anti-inflammatory and pain-relieving properties aid in the physical process of decluttering. It also relieves anxiety, which can rise up when you're clearing out objects to which you have an emotional attachment.

HOW TO

1. Enjoy your sacred herb as you assess why you're angry. Transforming that heated energy to clear your home of bad memories and clutter is a productive way to release your anger, an important form of spiritual self-care.
2. Grab a trash bag and toss in anything that triggers your anger. Be smart about it. For example, if your couch reminds you of your ex, but you can't afford a new couch, let the couch be. Items such as a past lover's clothing or office supplies from an old job can be donated whenever possible or thrown out.
3. Fight your anger with endorphins and adrenaline. Throw out old sheets after a breakup. Get rid of old condiments in the fridge. Toss out old makeup.
4. Did the exercise put you in a better mood while improving your home? Take a hit to celebrate.

20 MINUTES

Banish Self-Doubt

Benefits: You are love and light; you are talented and deserve all the love and success you want. These mantras will remind you that this is true, and banish any voices that say otherwise, by increasing your sense of inner peace, mindfulness, motivation, and positivity.

How does cannabis help? Thoughts of self-doubt frequently replay themselves as intrusive thoughts that feel like a twisted mantra. Cannabis will help silence the unwanted self-doubting thought patterns and replace them with mantras of confidence.

HOW TO

1. You will need paper, a pen, something soft to sit on such as a pillow or yoga mat, and your cannabis. Sit down. Enjoy some cannabis to silence unwanted thoughts and make space for encouraging ones.
2. Begin writing an intention letter. This letter should state what you want to release and what you want to manifest, so as you work to banish self-doubt, describe what has you questioning yourself. Do you feel that you're unworthy of a job or the career of your dreams? Perhaps a former partner made you feel bad about yourself? Get those nasty thoughts out of your head and onto paper. Then, start writing about what you want. Describe your ideal career coming true (it can). Write about your perfect partner or family.

3. When you finish writing your intention letter, read it back to yourself. Focusing on the affirmative aspect of what you wish to manifest, boil it down to one concise and action-oriented sentence stated in the present tense. It may be something like "I am on my way to the career of my dreams," "I will meet the right partner," or "I deserve love and success." This phrase is your personal intention.
4. Get into lotus pose by sitting cross-legged and putting each foot on the opposite thigh. Place your hands on your thighs, opening upward to receive. Close your eyes and begin breathing intentionally to enter a meditative space.
5. After a few moments, begin chanting your intention. Say it out loud, over and over. When your intuition says it's time to stop, complete a few more cycles of breath and then continue to go about your day.
6. Continue to recite your intention. Saying it out loud is extra therapeutic, but you can mentally repeat it on your commute, when you're feeling anxious, or anytime you need a confidence boost.

30 MINUTES (WHENEVER YOU'RE READY)

Forgive Someone

***Benefits*:** If someone caused you deep pain, you do not have to allow them back into your life, and you also deserve to live free of the pain of anger. This exercise allows you to fully feel your anger, from a safe space, and then let it go—an act that can lead to lowered anxiety, improved self-esteem, and a more uplifting feeling in your soul.

How does cannabis help? Deciding to forgive someone who deeply hurt you is brave—but stressful. Of all the medical uses of cannabis, stress management is one of the most common. Cannabis will keep you calm and lower anxiety levels as you step into forgiveness.

HOW TO

1. Before you begin this exercise, remember that forgiveness can't be rushed. If someone you trusted and loved hurt you, you are allowed to take your time to feel pain, anger, and sadness. As time passes, these feelings will lessen in intensity. There will come a day when you're not as invested in the pain, and perhaps even have compassion for this person. This may mean it's time to forgive. If you're not there yet, that's okay. Reflecting on your feelings and waiting until you're ready to forgive is its own act of self-care.
2. If you find that you are ready to forgive, sit down with a pen and paper. Consume some cannabis to lower anxiety and stress. Taking marijuana hits as needed to soothe your nerves,

begin writing this person a letter. It can be as messy and emotional and typo-ridden as you like.

3. Write out everything you feel. Write the ways that person hurt or betrayed you and how that affected your life. Write down what you wish you could say to their face. If it feels right, apologize for the ways that you may have hurt them to let that baggage go as well.
4. Finally, explain that you forgive them. Perhaps write a few sentences about what you appreciated about them and how you wish them a happy future.
5. Send the letter, hold onto it while you think about it, or keep it for your eyes only. Burn it if you want!
6. Finally, act on your decision to forgive. Let go, practice compassion, and allow yourself the joy of life beyond the pain this person caused you.

Dress Up in Something Over the Top

Benefits: When you try something new, such as an outfit or look that you worry that you can't pull off, you face your fears and overcome them, which will help you embrace boldness, see a new side of yourself, and stimulate creativity—all powerful acts of self-care that are good for your soul.

How does cannabis help? Cannabis raises dopamine levels in your brain, which will help you become more fearless and less inhibited. When in a high state of mind, you're more likely to say yes to what you truly want—such as wearing an over-the-top outfit or trying a new look—and less likely to feel self-conscious.

HOW TO

1. We all have an outrageous style icon. Maybe it's Lady Gaga and her unpredictable gowns. Perhaps it's David Bowie and his famous ever-evolving looks. Identify what you long to wear but worry you can't pull off and obtain it (if you don't already own it). Thrift shops are ideal for finding affordable and out-there clothing.
2. After you have your outfit sit down and smoke some marijuana. Text all your friends and plan a night out, then put on some music, ideally a playlist or record that mirrors the vibe of the outfit you will wear.
3. As the herb washes over you, lowering inhibitions and increasing confidence, remind yourself that the only trick to pulling an outfit off is putting it on. Then, with the music blaring

and your plans in place, put on your outfit. Do your hair and makeup to match. You are holding back on nothing tonight and using the magic of glamour and cannabis to be as bold and confident as possible.

4. Before you go out, have an edible to maintain a lifted mind. You can dance high all night without worrying about smoke or sneaking anything into a club. Share with friends.
5. Dance with your crew, make out with someone new, and enjoy feeling (and looking) fabulous.

AT LEAST 30 MINUTES

Pause to Process Tough Emotions

***Benefits*:** When difficult emotions or bad news hit, your first response may be to panic and make rash and impulsive decisions. In these situations the human body tells you that you are at risk and must fix things immediately! This emotional processing ritual allows you to practice self-care by taking the time to step back, center yourself, and proceed in a calm, rational state.

How does cannabis help? Many cannabis users report increased mindfulness, or enhanced ability to stay in the moment, while using this sacred herb. Additionally, cannabis is known to create calm. These properties help you pause and sit still so you can process tough emotions before acting on impulse. For this spiritual self-care exercise, choose an intake method that works quickly, such as a bong, dabs, a joint, or a bowl. You want to feel cannabis's immediate effects in a time of panic.

HOW TO

1. Bad things happen. It's part of life for everyone and, unfortunately, pain often brings up intense emotions, such as fear, sadness, remorse, anger, guilt, shame, and betrayal. Understandably, such news and emotions may trigger a panic response, which may cause you to make some impulsive decisions that you'll regret later. So before you act rashly, consume some cannabis.

2. After you smoke, notice how you feel calmer and sedated. Put down your electronics for now. Sit somewhere you feel comfortable and safe. Without worrying about following any meditation structure, focus on inhaling and exhaling. Consume more cannabis as needed.
3. Take a moment to assess your physical safety. Are you okay? Can you feel the ground? Is there any immediate danger? Remind yourself that you are safe.
4. Stay in the present. What do you know about the situation upsetting you? Focus on the facts and ban any gossip from affecting your perception of events.
5. Take a moment to reflect on all that you've survived in your life. Have you been through worse than this? Has someone you know? Did you come out okay? You can do it again. This will pass.
6. Give yourself at least 30 minutes to feel grounded and calm before making any major decisions. Then, when you're less likely to act on blind emotion, put together a support system of family, friends, and your therapist. With their help, put together a plan.

10 MINUTES OR SO

Stay Present at a Social Event

Benefits: Staying in the present, or experiencing mindfulness, allows you to inhabit each moment of life fully, which is a powerful way to practice spiritual self-care. Additionally, research suggests that mindfulness decreases anxiety, reduces distractions, and improves mental cognition.

How does cannabis help? Science shows that cannabis can help fight anxiety, and it's also a terrific tool for keeping you focused and in the present moment. This mindfulness ritual uses cannabis to help you clear your brain of past or future worries and stay in the moment so you can fully experience the right now; it can be practiced anytime or during a potentially stressful social event. For this self-care exercise, use a strain of cannabis that helps you stay present in social situations, perhaps an activating sativa if you're easily distracted, or a relaxing CBD-heavy indica if you're prone to anxiety.

HOW TO

1. Discreetly bring your portable cannabis kit (see Create a Cannabis-on-the-Go Kit in Part 2) with you to social events, be it a date or party. This way you are prepared whenever you begin to find yourself lost in the clouds, anxious, or mentally escaping from the present even though you're thrilled to be there.
2. Should you find yourself drifting away and struggling to focus during a conversation with your friends, new people, or your date, politely excuse yourself.

3. Step outside where you can safely smoke or vape and take a few hits of this sacred herb. As the effects take hold, use your five senses to ground yourself in the present and get out of your head. What can you smell? Cannabis? The scent of your city? What do you see? Street signs, people walking, dogs, trees? What can you hear? Music, cars, conversation? What can you touch? The fabric of your purse or wallet, the smoothness of your pipe, the wind against your face? What can you taste? Cannabis? When you feel that you're mindful of your present, head back in.
4. As you return to the social function, make it your mission to stay present. Focus on cues such as a friend's voice, the music, or lighting to hold on to. Use cannabis to tell yourself you're on a mindfulness mission. Once you are fully immersed, it will be easier to stay there.

10 MINUTES, PLUS THE LENGTH OF A DATE

Focus On Your Partner

Benefits: Focusing on your partner allows you to listen and learn about their wants and needs. It helps you care for someone you love and give them attention and joy. Becoming tuned into their desires will enable you to be the best partner possible, which they will then reciprocate.

How does cannabis help? Cannabis is known to increase empathy and mindfulness. It helps you move into a giving place in your heart, so you can focus on the person you love. It also facilitates deep conversations in which you can listen, learn, and laugh with your partner.

HOW TO

1. Whenever you start to feel distant from your partner take 10 minutes out of your busy day to prioritize your relationship as a type of meditative self-care. Sit comfortably and slowly inhale cannabis, and then exhale cannabis. Repeat as desired and then move to normal intentional breathing.
2. Begin mentally creating a gratitude list of things you appreciate about your partner. This can include the love and support they provide you, their smell, their passion for their job, their taste in music, and so much more. Consider what's going on in your partner's life right now. Is there family drama, work stress, or some other life event that is a source of anxiety? Ask yourself what you can do to be supportive and to make space for their needs.

3. With your cannabis in tow, so you and your partner can enjoy it together, find some quality time to spend with your partner. Continue to focus on all the reasons why you love and appreciate them. Share the reasons you appreciate them that came to you during your earlier meditation. Do your best to avoid common distraction behaviors such as interrupting, becoming mentally distracted by work worries, or pretending to listen when you're actually waiting for your turn to speak.
4. If you're in a place where touch is appropriate, pay attention to your partner's body language, and ask them what they need. Perhaps they have a stiff neck and could use a shoulder rub. They may desire hugs and kisses and other physical displays of attention.
5. Light up the ganja. Notice how you feel joy due to your partner's pleasure and how focusing on them instead of yourself is a mutually beneficial gift. Watch your conversation erupt into laughter with the aid of Mary Jane.

AT LEAST 30 MINUTES

Write an Apology

Benefits: Writing an apology cannot undo an action. However, an apology can help the person you hurt, and it can help you move past any shame or guilt that kept you stuck in the past, leaving you feeling lighter and free and able to move forward.

How does cannabis help? Writing an apology can be an emotionally painful experience, but the emotional processing and mood-stabilizing properties of cannabis, in particular CBD, can ground you and make writing the letter easier.

HOW TO

1. Take a moment to smoke cannabis and ground yourself. Once you feel calm, reflect on what you are apologizing for. Do the difficult work of putting yourself in the other person's shoes and using empathy to consider how your actions affected them.
2. Sit at your computer and begin typing. If you aren't sure how to start your letter, begin typing anyway. Eventually the right words will begin to flow, and you can always go back and edit later. Your apology should address how you messed up, state your remorse, illustrate how you will make amends for your actions, and state what you have learned. Make sure your letter hits all these points. Keep your cannabis nearby. Marijuana works wonders for encouraging creativity and fighting writer's block.

3. When you're ready, send the apology. You can email it, use snail mail, or depending on your relationship with this person, call and use your letter to help you give a verbal apology.
4. You must leave the next step up to the person you hurt. They are allowed to need time and space, and if they don't want you in their life, you must respect that. It doesn't mean that your apology wasn't an important and honorable act of self-care that provided comfort to both parties.
5. Promise yourself that now that you've apologized, you will stop beating yourself up. Use this mistake to become a better person (see Forgive Yourself in this part).

AT LEAST 20 MINUTES

Take a Sound Bath

Benefits: Sound baths, a musical experience most often created by singing bowls, gongs, and tuning forks, direct the mind to conscious relaxation. They work to decrease stress, promote healing and meditation, and align the body, mind, and spirit.

How does cannabis help? Cannabis, especially heavy indicas and properly dosed edibles, helps you sink fully into your body. This sacred herb not only heightens senses, such as sound perception, but blurs them. A sound bath can invoke stunning visuals that add to your elevated meditation.

HOW TO

1. Obtain your form of sound and cannabis. You can put together an organized sound bath with friends or play a singing bowl yourself while in a seated meditation. If you're solo and want to lie down, you can find instrumental tracks or *YouTube* videos of Tibetan singing bowls. You can also purchase them at yoga and new age shops or online.
2. Sit or lie down on your yoga mat, pillow, or blanket. Take out your marijuana and inhale and exhale mindfully. Let the effects wash over your body. As you begin to elevate into cannabis-induced relaxation, start playing your singing bowl, press play on your music, or let your friend leading the meditation start. To use a singing bowl, press the accompanying mallet in a circular motion against the bowl's outer rim. You should hear a sharp, bright tone. Slow down for a gentler

experience. Put your whole body into the motion and adjust speed as flows naturally.

3. Focus on the sound vibrations. Using the creative properties of cannabis, imagine your entire being bathed in the sacred light. Surrender to it. Feel it permeate your body. Keep your eyes closed and notice what visions arise in your mind. Let the sounds carry you away from worries and into a trancelike state. Use the music as your lighthouse to direct you back to serenity when the mind begins to wander.
4. Slowly come back to an awakened state. If you can, take it easy the rest of the day to absorb the experience and revel in your self-care.

Create Your Own Cannabis Sanctuary

Benefits: Creating a dedicated space, or altar, provides you with a safe space to worship and honor. Cannabis is worthy of both. With a cannabis sanctuary, you don't have to arrange pillows and smoking supplies every time you wish to do a meditation or breathing exercise or to chill; all you have to do is relax.

How does cannabis help? Cannabis increases dopamine levels in the brain, which not only helps us pay attention and keep on task for activities that involve organization, but also turns such tasks into fun adventures. Its creative properties will help you create a unique sanctuary attuned to your needs.

HOW TO

1. Designate a space in your home for a cannabis sanctuary. It can be an entire room or a corner of your bedroom. The only qualification is that your cannabis sanctuary must be a place of calm where you can be alone.
2. Partake in cannabis to focus your mind and get your creative juices flowing. Look at the space as a blank slate ready to be transformed into art. What does your ideal cannabis sanctuary look like? Is it glittery and glamorous? Is it minimally decorated and a sacred space of reflection? Is it cozy and filled with items and images that make you feel safe? Use your pen and notepad to sketch out a quick diagram of a cannabis sanctuary that you'll look forward to spending time in.

3. Gather your supplies, which may include a pillow, blanket, or yoga mat to sit on, your cannabis supplies (see Organize Your Cannabis Supplies in Part 2), a music source, sage or incense for aromatherapy and to mask odors, a notebook and pen to write down ideas, and a space for crafts. If you have cannabis art or photos to decorate your sanctuary with, collect those as well.
4. Get to work! Place your cannabis supplies on a table or tray. Adorn the space with decorations, from images of cannabis to band posters and photographs—anything that inspires you. Set up your yoga mat, pillow, or blanket on the floor for meditation. Have fun creating a space that's sacred to you.
5. When you're done, consummate the space by lighting up in your sanctuary. Now you have a welcoming space that's filled with everything you need for cannabis self-care rituals.

Watch a Sunset

***Benefits*:** Time spent with nature is shown to boost vitality. Watching a sunset is a (free) way to let the beauty of nature heal your soul while also practicing mindfulness. One study says that awe-inspiring sights like sunsets increase your concern for others, so you're more likely to care for loved ones.

How does cannabis help? THC's focusing properties are a mindfulness tool that will keep you off your phone and enjoying the colorful view. The view of the sunset may evoke a song in your mind, or it may seem like you can taste the colors, as cannabis not only enhances senses but blends them.

HOW TO

1. Pack cannabis in a form appropriate for consumption where you'll be watching the sunset.
2. Arrive early, before the sun begins to set. Puff on your cannabis as the sun begins its slow crawl below the horizon.
3. If you can, stay for the entire show, until the sun dips below the horizon and nighttime begins.
4. Let your senses come alive and mingle together as you watch the Earth's beautiful bedtime ritual. Feel a sense of calm wash over you as you experience this soul-soothing act of self-care.

ABOUT 10 MINUTES

Pause to Honor This Sacred Herb

Benefits: Taking the time to observe and honor cannabis makes you more mindful and therefore grateful for its psychedelic properties. The cannabis you smoke is from female plants known as sinsemilla. Understanding what forms the colorful buds take and how they work enhances both your marijuana knowledge and appreciation.

How does cannabis help? Cannabis intensifies the senses. Your admiration for the buds of a cannabis plant is amplified when your senses of smell, taste, and sight are also enhanced. Marijuana also affects our perception of time, so just a few minutes of reflective self-care feels like hours of wisdom gained.

HOW TO

1. Find a quiet place where you can sit. Then smoke a bowl or joint using your strain of choice.
2. As you inhale and exhale, focus on the taste. What does your cannabis taste like? If you're having a sativa, such as Lemon Haze, you'll notice notes of clean, sharp citrus and a grounding earthy flavor. An indica like Bubba Kush may remind you more of candy than sharp lemon with its sweet flavor profile.
3. Once you're happily elevated, take the remaining buds out and bring them up to your nose. What does the bud smell like? Is it similar to the taste? Is it woody, or does it remind you of your favorite pie? You're familiar with the smell of cannabis smoke, but the smell of buds can vary plant to plant.

4. Examine the buds. The crystal-like formations covering the bud are called resin, or kief. Resin is from trichomes, clear potent hairs that ooze terpenes, the fragrant oils responsible for how the plant smells. Trichomes also produce the cannabinoids that give marijuana its magic powers. Take a moment to thank terpenes for secreting such an awesome and important oil.
5. What color are your buds? Depending on the light and temperature the plant is exposed to, the cannabis buds can be green, orange, purple, and even black (goth weed). Colors usually begin to come in and change in the second half of the flowering stage.
6. Sit with your buds gently in your hand and give thanks to this plant. Vow to notice the varying characteristics of buds moving forward to respect and honor Mary Jane, and know that there is an extremely safe plant medicine readily available to nourish your soul.

AT LEAST 10 MINUTES

Find Your Confidence

Benefits: The self-confidence you'll gain from this self-care exercise will increase your performance in both professional and personal settings. Flipping your mood from afraid to confident completely changes your outlook, and a positive outlook leads to a positive outcome.

How does cannabis help? Cannabis is linked to increased self-esteem and confidence as the plant can open your mind to new perspectives. Cannabis also lowers anxiety and stress levels, creating a mind-set more conducive to confidence. Since you want to raise confidence and lower anxiety and self-doubt, opt for a strain high in CBD.

HOW TO

1. For this exercise, you will need music, a meditation pillow, and cannabis. Sit comfortably on your meditation pillow and turn on some music. The music should be made up of songs that help boost your mood and self-esteem, written by an artist who inspires you to be your best self.
2. Spend a few minutes reflecting on your self-doubt and why it's unhelpful, as you chill with your cannabis.
3. Begin listing, out loud or in your head, personal achievements. These can be as big as a promotion or as small as completing a difficult yoga class. Continue to check off your successes for as long as you like.

4. Now simply sit and let the music run through you. Get amped. If this musician can act so confidently and enjoy such earthly rewards, so can you.
5. Begin chanting the phrase "I got this." At first, it may feel weak and afraid. Continue chanting along with the music until the words no longer feel foreign, but mundane, even boring. Of course you've got this!
6. Thanks to the music, cannabis, mantra, and meditation, you should be feeling terrific. Do not hold back if you want to get up and dance or pretend to be your patron rock star.
7. Return to your day feeling—and knowing—that you got this! And that you have an inner rock star ready to come by, light up a joint, and kick self-doubt to the curb whenever you need a confidence boost.

Share Stories with Friends

Benefits: Storytelling will help you piece together memories from your past and emotionally process those experiences with your friends. Sharing your story, as well as listening to ones others are telling, will help you forge connections (an important self-care activity) and deepen your bonds.

How does cannabis help? Cannabis is linked to self-expression and introspection, and it will lower your inhibitions as you share your personal history with others.

HOW TO

1. Pick a date and plan a cannabis storytelling night. Invite close friends whom you trust. Let them know you're having a chill cannabis night with storytelling and games.
2. Prepare for the event. If you have access to outdoors, make a bonfire (see Build a Campfire in this part). Sitting around the fire telling stories is a human pastime that goes back centuries. If you don't have a place to build a fire, create an intimate, cozy space indoors. Place pillows on the floor for people to sit on so you create a circular setup. This way everyone can see and be seen and hear and be heard.
3. Stock up on munchies and beverages. Depending on your budget, provide the cannabis or mention in the invite that it's BYOB (bring your own bud).
4. While cannabis tends to encourage storytelling on its own, for fun and to help focus the night, write down prompts and

place them in a bowl for people to pick out. These could include: Who was your first love? What is your most terrifying memory? What is your favorite memory involving music? What is your favorite memory involving cannabis?

5. Use cannabis to stay present. Sometimes when a friend is telling a story, you may not pay attention because you're going over in your mind what you want to say next. Utilize the mindfulness properties of cannabis to listen with intention as others speak. Likewise, when it's your turn, be fully present in your body and mind, mentally shielded from disruptions.
6. Notice how relationships shape and change throughout sharing stories. You may find yourself hitting it off with someone unexpected as they reveal a new side of themselves.

Appreciate a Rainy Day

Benefits: Rainy days keep us inside, which can help us get work done or take care of chores around the house. But if you have nothing to do, staying inside on a rainy day keeps you cozy to hang out with friends, family, or pets, or offers an excuse for much-needed alone time that can be used to practice self-care.

How does cannabis help? Cannabis heightens your senses. The sound of rain becomes even more soothing, as does the fresh scent created when the raindrops hit the ground. Rather than feel trapped inside, you can take advantage of the productive, creative energy that you'll feel thanks to the increase of dopamine that cannabis causes, while at the same time the CBD in cannabis will encourage calm and relaxation.

HOW TO

1. When you wake up to rain, take your time as much as possible, following the lead of nature. Add cannabis to your morning ritual. If you're able, once you're awake and calm yet focused, simply sit with the showers. Relish the sound of raindrops splattering on the ground and any thunder. Look out the window and watch the grey clouds opening up, the pouring of water from the sky. Open a window and inhale the unmistakable smell of raindrops. Think of all the plants and animals that will benefit from the rain.

2. What do you have to do today? If there is work and chores to be done consider how much you can get accomplished with such calming background sounds.
3. If you have a free day, how would you like to use it? Rainy days are perfect for spending time with friends and family. Even if you live alone, it's an opportunity to call and catch up with loved ones—calls to family and friends are said to go up when it's raining.
4. Relish all the ways you get to practice self-care with cannabis on a rainy day. You can use it in a meditation, you can chill out on your couch and watch movies, or you can use the day to bake some edibles.
5. Whatever is right for you, give thanks to the Earth for this rainy day. Whether it was chores, time with friends, television, or baking—you utilized the day as it was meant for you.
6. When the rain stops, make sure to go outside or open a window to look at the beautiful sky (there may be rainbows!) and enjoy the petrichor, the fresh, pleasant scent of Earth after a rainfall.

AT LEAST AN HOUR

Forgive Yourself

Benefits: This act of self-care asks you to sit with difficult emotions and then forgive yourself and let any shame or disappointment go. Releasing these difficult emotions is a true exercise in self-care that can lead to self-love and decreased stress and anxiety levels.

How does cannabis help? Cannabis, in particular the cannabinoid CBD, can help you face difficult subjects and emotions from a calm place of positivity. Cannabis also facilitates a perspective shift, and helps you feel more empathetic toward yourself, consciously analyze what you can learn, and also relax, let go, and lighten up.

HOW TO

1. As a human being it is inevitable that you will make mistakes and hurt someone you love. While it's crucial to accept responsibility, apologize, and grow, staying in a swamp of shame is counterproductive and harmful. When you feel strong enough to forgive yourself and move on, obtain some cannabis high in CBD.
2. Smoke the cannabis somewhere peaceful where you can reflect on what happened, where you went wrong, how you can help make it better, and what you can learn. Make a note of what you learned. It may be the importance of honesty or sticking to your word. Decide to hold yourself accountable and live in a way that reflects such change going forward.

3. On a piece of paper, for your eyes only, write down everything you feel bad about. Take every last drop of guilt and shame, two nasty emotions, and spill it onto the paper with ink. Consume cannabis as needed when difficult emotions become intolerable.
4. When your letter of guilt is finished, rip it to shreds and throw them away. Take this as more than a symbolic gesture. The time for beating yourself up is over. Now you must move on with life using the lessons learned.
5. Finally, to relax and literally detox, take a hot bath filled with bath salts. Smoke a joint while in the bath to unwind. Remind yourself of your positive qualities and look forward to a future in which you are wiser than you were yesterday.

VARIES FROM SITUATION TO SITUATION

Indulge In a Guilty Pleasure

Benefits: Outlawing something that you enjoy, be it eating an entire pint of ice cream, binge-watching TV shows, or sleeping past noon, doesn't remove desire. While you shouldn't make unhealthy habits a daily part of your life, indulging in a guilty pleasure prevents it from becoming an obsession and acts as a healthy type of soulful self-care.

How does cannabis help? From the visuals of a TV show to the taste of a frozen dessert, cannabis makes your guilty pleasures feel even better by enhancing your sensory abilities. It will help you stop being embarrassed by indulging and start embracing joy.

HOW TO

1. Feel the right time to dig into a guilty pleasure. Perhaps you had a stressful week and need some joy. Or maybe you just got some great news and you want to celebrate. You're ready to treat yourself.
2. Whether it's a TV show, cake, or your favorite cocktail, sit down with your guilty pleasure and your cannabis.
3. Notice how your body lights up and your senses become heightened. Make yourself wait a little longer to indulge in your guilty pleasure as you enjoy your cannabis.
4. Finally, turn on the show, eat the cake, or take a sip of your cocktail. Appreciate how cannabis enhances even your guilty pleasure and luxuriate in this seemingly sinful type of self-care.

AT LEAST 20 MINUTES

Stare at the Stars

Benefits**:** Staring up at the stars provides a healthy perspective shift that reminds you how immense the universe is. It's an awe-inspiring way to connect with nature and alleviate stress and worries.

How does cannabis help? Cannabis enhances the senses. The gorgeous starry sky becomes more visually appealing. The quiet of nature becomes exceedingly silent. The mind-expanding properties of cannabis amplify your perspective shift and make this spiritual self-care act even more powerful.

HOW TO

1. Go somewhere you can see the stars. Depending on where you live this may be your backyard, the beach, or a campground as part of a planned camping trip.
2. Consume cannabis. As the herb expands your mind and enhances your senses, look up at the sky. Reflect on how you are simultaneously insignificant yet sacredly significant as you gaze at the universe.
3. Admire the twinkling stars and vivid planets, and keep your eyes peeled for a shooting star. How does the moon look? If you're stargazing under a full moon, admire its greatness; if you're admiring the new moon, look for the darkest starry sky possible.
4. Stay fully present. When it's time to pack up, carry the perspective gained back to your daily life and appreciate the balm this self-care ritual has put on your soul.

Attend a Comedy Show

Benefits: Comedy makes you laugh and laughter reduces stress, lifts your mood, and relieves pain by prompting the release of endorphins.

How does cannabis help? Studies show that cannabis stimulates blood flow to the right frontal and left temporal lobes of your brain, the areas responsible for laughter, which helps explain why cannabis encourages laughter. Edibles are an ideal method of consumption for a night out at a comedy show because they'll likely kick in right as the comedy starts. If you want to bring more with you, edibles are a discreet way to go out with cannabis.

HOW TO

1. Plan your comedy night. Check listings at your local comedy clubs and grab tickets to an event that speaks to you. If you are unfamiliar with who is coming to town, get high and check out each comedian's social media and *YouTube* videos to get a sense of their vibe. Invite your friends along, so you can bond over a gut-busting night out.
2. Ingest your edibles, then head to the show. Arrange a safe method of transportation, so all you have to worry about is getting high and having fun.
3. Kick back at the comedy show. Relish the sensations of the edible kicking in—relax into the body high and let your mind go. Your only job is to sit back and enjoy the show. This is

your night off, and it's time to laugh. There is no need to be self-conscious; the entire point of a comedy show is to laugh.

4. After the show, either in person or online through social media, let the comedians know how much you enjoyed the show. They are hardworking people too, and it's good karma!
5. Bask in the post-show joy and giggles and let your good mood flow into the next day.

AT LEAST 20 MINUTES

Spend Time with Your Role Models

Benefits: Connecting with a role model, be it a rock star, family member (deceased or otherwise), or a colleague, will inspire and motivate you to become the best version of yourself. It reminds you that just like them, you can accomplish your dreams and not only survive, but prosper, after hard times.

How does cannabis help? A study shows that cannabis encourages divergent thinking, or a way to come up with creative ideas by considering a multitude of solutions. Divergent thinking expands your imagination and helps you use rock lyrics to learn a lesson, or pray to your deceased grandmother under the possibility that she's listening.

HOW TO

1. Smoke some cannabis, ideally a strain that aids in creativity, such as Willie Nelson, a sativa lauded for its creative properties and appropriately named after a great artist and role model to many.
2. Reflect on who your role model is and why you admire them. Do they have a strong work ethic? Are they fearlessly themselves? Do they create music or art that inspires you and gives you joy?
3. Take action to connect with them. If they are alive and someone you know, call them up and ask for advice on a situation you're struggling with. If it's a deceased relative, talk to them; it's okay if you're not religious or into prayer. You're just talking

to your grandma. If it's a rock star or other artist, put on music or engage with whatever form of art they created.

4. Despite how different the scenarios may be depending on your role model, remember that we are all striving for the same goal: We want to connect with our role model and their character traits that inspire us and use that to become more aware of our personal power. If you actually spoke with someone, integrate their advice into actions you can take to better yourself. When speaking with a deceased family member, you can say literally anything, because, well, they're dead, so they can't gossip. As you're sharing, with a mind open wide thanks to cannabis, you will notice their advice filling your brain, bringing comfort and clarity. And if your role model is a famous artist find yourself in their music, paintings, or films.
5. Finally, cap off this self-care ritual by reminding yourself that if your role model can become that successful and inspiring, so can you.

15 MINUTES OR SO

Exchange Affirmations with a Friend

Benefits: Studies show that positive affirmations promote better psychological well-being, increase performance under stress, and activate the reward circuit of the brain. And spending time with your friends can help relieve stress and increase your self-esteem.

How does cannabis help? The release of feel-good dopamine provided by cannabis helps you open your heart, which makes it easier to be vulnerable and emotive around others. It also silences your inner critic and acts as a reward.

HOW TO

1. Invite a trusted friend over for cannabis and chill. You can either ask them before they come if they want to share positive affirmations or bring it up in the moment. For the latter, simply ask, "Want to take turns complimenting each other?" Who can say no to that?
2. Once your friend arrives, share a joint or bowl, something you can pass back and forth.
3. Go first. Think of something sincere, and then tell your friend, "You show up for people in times of need," or another pertinent affirmation. When they affirm you, believe them.
4. As the joint burns on, it's okay, even encouraged, if affirmations become sillier, such as, "You can pull off any hair color."
5. Thank your friend for their words and appreciate the way this intimate form of self-care can nourish you.

AT LEAST 20 MINUTES

Banish Cannabis Stigma and Shame

***Benefits*:** Despite ongoing legalization, many of us were taught stoner stereotypes about cannabis. As a result, you may feel a sense of shame over using cannabis, even though it's no different (and even safer) than drinking wine. Don't let those outdated stereotypes make you feel bad about enjoying cannabis and using it to become your best self. This self-care exercise will help you see how releasing that shame can give you a healthy perspective and the motivation to live your best life.

How does cannabis help? Cannabis's ability to help you think in a multitude of ways (divergent thinking) allows you to replace outdated shame-ridden thoughts with accurate, current knowledge. And the lowered inhibitions that cannabis brings make it easier to love yourself.

HOW TO

1. Consume your favorite cannabis in your preferred way.
2. To remove shame and stigma, we must first expose it. Using a pen and paper, write out any outdated tidbits about cannabis that are impeding your ability to embrace the plant fully. This list could include the word "lazy" or other terms historically used to negatively portray cannabis users.
3. Consider where your shame originated. Perhaps it's outdated drug knowledge you learned at school that has since been debunked. Identifying the root of shame helps you understand and let it go.

4. Grab your lighter, then burn the list of shame in a fire-safe location (perhaps over the sink or in a backyard fire pit). It is gone.
5. Head back to your writing space. Now that all fires are out, and the shame is gone, it's time to celebrate. Consume some more cannabis!
6. Take out a new blank page of paper and write what you like about cannabis and how it's helped you. This can range from medical-based info such as "I have less social anxiety and more friends now" or "I can treat my back pain at home" to sillier things such as "I dance better to Snoop Dogg."

Build a Campfire

Benefits: Building a campfire is a survival skill that's also a workout. Creating one and taking the time to enjoy it allows you to nourish your spirit by connecting with your friends and family and sharing stories and joints.

How does cannabis help? Cannabis enhances the senses. Use them to connect with the outdoors and the flame you've created, and use your heightened sense of beauty to watch it burn. For this self-care ritual, wait until the fire is burning to light up.

HOW TO

1. Collect your supplies. You'll need matches, tinder, kindling, logs, and water to put the fire out. Lighter fluid is unnecessary and can be dangerous.
2. Choose a location that is away from trees, woods, or anything flammable. If you're at a campsite, there are likely premade firepits, or maybe you have a firepit in your own backyard. If not, select a space on bare earth away from grass and remove other flammable bits of nature. Dig a hole to contain the wood and keep it away from the seating area.
3. Take your tinder (leaves, twigs, wood shavings, dry grass, or other small flammable bits) and place it in the center of your pit.
4. Take your larger kindling, wood that is bigger than sticks but much smaller than logs, and form a teepee shape around your tinder. Place more wood downwind than upwind and leave

an upwind opening to light the fire. This way, the smoke won't blow straight into everyone's face.

5. Create a bigger teepee using your logs.
6. Light a match and place it on top of the tinder to light the fire. Light additional spots as needed. Then watch the flame spread until it reaches the outer logs and forms a glorious fire.
7. Light up your cannabis, begin passing it around the fire, and share stories with your friends and family, nourishing your spirit and engaging in important self-care.

10 MINUTES

Take a Sunbath

***Benefits*:** Short-term exposure to sunlight gives you vitamin D, the nutrient your body needs to absorb calcium. Even small doses of sunlight can boost mood and satisfy your spirit by connecting it with the power of nature.

How does cannabis help? CBD contains mood-stabilizing and anti-depressant properties, so allow your sunbath to help you relax and soothe your soul. Cannabis heightens senses, including touch, and will amplify the comforting feeling of the sun's warmth.

HOW TO

1. On a sunny day, when you need a mood lift, pack a joint, water, and a blanket or towel and head to your backyard, roof, or a nearby park.
2. Lie down and relax. Puff on your joint as you feel the warmth of the sun surrounding your body. Let your imagination run wild contemplating the glory of our planet and the sun, our solar system's star.
3. After 10 minutes in the sun rays, head indoors or apply a minimum of SPF 30 sunscreen and continue to boost your spirit with this warming act of self-care.

15 MINUTES

Perform a Cord-Cutting Ritual

Benefits: Cord cutting is a powerful, soul-expanding ritual that empowers you to sever emotional ties with someone who is no longer a healthy part of your life. Taking action to release yourself from a toxic or damaged relationship is freeing. Cord cutting creates closure, so you can move onto new relationships that help you flourish.

How does cannabis help? This self-care ritual asks you to rely on your imagination to visualize a cord connecting you and the person you need to cut ties with. Cannabis enhances your visualization abilities and helps you release hurt and begin to heal wounds.

HOW TO

1. Curate a tranquil environment with minimal distractions. Grab your cannabis. Sit on your meditation pillow or yoga mat.
2. As you smoke, think about who you are cutting cords with and why. Is it a friend who is acting cruel toward you, or an ex-romantic partner who still takes up too much room in your mind? Closure is not something gained over coffee, but an active decision you make to move forward with your life. It happens within. Cord cutting does not mean you are banishing this person for good. It's like trimming your hair. You must cut off the dead ends so healthy hair can grow.

3. Put down your cannabis and close your eyes. First, visualize yourself. Mentally scan yourself from your head to your toes, so you have a copy of yourself in your mind.
4. Now visualize the other person as if they are sitting across from you. Imagine them in as much detail as possible, from their face to what they're wearing, down to their shoes.
5. Imagine a cord connecting your heart to theirs. This represents your current relationship. While healthy cords are usually vibrant colors, as this is a painful situation the cord may appear grey, black, or whatever imagery your mind associates with hurt.
6. Now visualize a pair of scissors. Take the scissors and with all your might snip the cord.
7. If this person is meant to come back into your life they can do so with a fresh start. If not, remind yourself that healthy love exists and that you deserve it.
8. Open your eyes and focus on a feeling of freedom.

AN HOUR OR SO

Walk Through a Cemetery

***Benefits*:** Strolling through a cemetery will help you reflect on the fleeting nature of life. A healthy reminder of death encourages you to look forward to the future, put things in perspective, and weigh out what's really important in this limited time you have on Earth.

How does cannabis help? Studies suggest that both CBD and THC act as mood boosters. While cemeteries are beautiful, they can bring up painful emotions. Cannabis provides a cushion so you can enjoy your cemetery experience with maximum benefits and minimal discomfort.

HOW TO

1. Pick a cemetery nearby and plan an afternoon with beautiful weather to go. You can venture alone if you require contemplation and solitude or invite a friend if you feel company will make the experience more compelling.
2. Smoke up before you leave or eat some edibles. You don't want to smoke around graves as it can be disrespectful. Arrange safe transportation to the graveyard.
3. When you arrive, utilize your heightened senses and take in nature. If you live in a city, cemeteries offer quiet and a chance to spend time in nature away from the concrete jungle.
4. Take your time and wander. Look around at all the graves. Each one represents a human, just like you, who loved, felt pain, worked, and laughed. Notice the flowers on top of

graves and the side-by-side plots of couples. These people were loved and loved in return.

5. Know that you will die one day too. Take a moment to sit down under a tree or wherever calls you. Ponder the idea that fearing death is useless as it's a non-negotiable part of life. The only effective way to live with this knowledge is to live a full and active life true to yourself. Ask yourself if you're building a legacy that leaves no stone unturned.
6. Do not fear death in the cemetery but appreciate the fact that you are alive. Notice the sensations on your body of being outside. Center yourself, give gratitude for your life, and make a promise to live your life in a manner that honors death.
7. If it's a graveyard where someone you know is buried, don't forget to say hi before you head home.

AT LEAST AN HOUR, AT YOUR OWN PACE

Explore a New Religion

Benefits: Learning about a new religion helps you understand not only its members but politics and history, which is useful to making sense of our modern world. Also, learning about another religion will expand your own capacities for love and understanding of others and may even inspire you.

How does cannabis help? A Harvard study found that cannabis can improve cognitive function. When pain is relieved and anxiety calmed, it is easier for the brain to learn and focus. Cannabis also opens the mind creatively to allow for nonjudgmental new ideas.

HOW TO

1. Consume cannabis and let your mind expand. Decide which religion interests you. What do you want to learn more about? Perhaps, as a cannabis connoisseur, you may be curious about Rastafarianism, a faith that believes cannabis is sacred.
2. Once you settle on an unfamiliar religion to explore, begin your research. Buy religious texts and books on the subject, as your desire and budget allows, but realize that the Internet provides a free plethora of information; just make sure to read reputable sources and stay away from anything biased or hateful. Read and learn with a notebook beside you so you can take notes as you go.
3. If you read something that you disagree with, use your elevated mind-set to remember that educating yourself on a

religion does not mean that you have to practice that religion or convert from a religion you may already be practicing. You don't have to associate yourself with any religion at all. You're just learning about something new. Conversely, if you learn something that resonates with you or inspires you, consider it a gift.

4. Reflect on how your new knowledge makes you feel. Inspired? Thoughtful? It is admirable that you now have a better understanding of a religion that was previously completely foreign to you. Notice how this knowledge aids you in day-to-day life.

Care for a Friend

Benefits: Caring for someone you love has been shown to lower stress and reduce blood pressure. It's also linked to increased self-esteem and self-worth, and it strengthens your connection with the recipient. Providing support for a loved one also helps you remember the depth of your relationships and that you're not alone. If the tables were turned, this person would care for you.

How does cannabis help? Cannabis encourages your brain to make connections and problem-solve, which will help you come up with solutions to care for a friend in need. The anxiety-, stress-, and depression-reducing properties of marijuana will help you stay calm, which can be useful as it can be challenging to see someone you care about struggle.

HOW TO

1. The next time a friend or loved one could use some help, reach out and ask if you can come over and take care of them. We all need loving care from time to time, and it need not be due to an emergency. While medical illnesses are an opportunity to take care of someone, so is a breakup, a death in the family, or a hard week at work. Perhaps your friend is feeling lonely and down and could use someone they trust to hang out with and help them with dinner.

2. If they're comfortable with you coming over, make sure to bring cannabis and any other items they request or that would be useful in their situation.
3. Ask your friend what you can do for them. Listen to what they say. Perhaps they want a shoulder rub with a cannabis topical, or to sit and watch a movie? Maybe they need someone to cook them a hot meal? Often people just want to be heard and feel less alone. Rather than try to fix the problem, or convince them into happiness, just listen and share empathy for what they are experiencing.
4. Break out the cannabis. If someone is in physical pain, non-psychoactive topicals can help relieve localized injury, as does consumption through edibles or inhalation. A few puffs of herbal goodness shared with a friend provides relief for everything from digestion issues to a broken heart.
5. When you head home, make sure to leave your friend with food and cannabis so they have self-care supplies when you're not there. Check in on them the next day.

Face Your Fears

Benefits: Facing your fears takes you outside of your comfort zone and proves that you can handle stress and feeling uncomfortable. You'll reap the rewards of courage, self-confidence, and pride that you faced your fears and came out thriving. Once you look your fear in the eye and survive, your soul will know its strength.

How does cannabis help? Cannabis lowers inhibitions, which helps you be yourself. In this self-care exercise the plant slays social anxiety, which may get in the way of many things you'd like to do but are scared to try.

HOW TO

1. Sit down with your cannabis on your yoga mat or meditation pillow. Light up and consume the cannabis. As your mind opens, meditate on the fear you'd like to face. For instance, you may have awful stage fright but want to be in a band. Perhaps you're scared of receiving love or putting yourself out there but you long for love.
2. After you've identified your fear, consider why it scares you. Are you scared you're going to do a lousy job or get rejected? Was there a time in your life in which you experienced shame or trauma that made you scared? Consider how many people successfully have what you want and remind yourself that you deserve it too.

3. When you finish meditating on the topic, reach out to someone you trust who has done the thing you've been afraid to do. Contact a friend who plays in a band or has a happy relationship. Offer to hang out and get them high so that you can pick their brain over a joint. Listen to the advice and insight they give.
4. When you're alone, elevate your mind, and complete any additional research on the topic. And then make it happen. Book your skydiving lessons, put out an ad for other musicians, ask your crush out. Boldness is powerful.
5. Do the activity. Face your fears. When you've finished, enjoy feeling confident, proud, and strong. If you can do that, what else can you do?

Further Resources

COMMON FAQS

Where can I safely obtain high-quality cannabis?

To start, make sure you're buying from a reputable dispensary. Online resources like *Weedmaps* and *Leafly* list and review dispensaries, as well as their strain list and inventory.

To maximize your cannabis experience, opt for the top-shelf variety at your local dispensary. Really good cannabis is also referred to as "loud," as opposed to "schwag," which means poor-quality buds. Your medical marijuana doctor or budtender is the best place to start, as they can help you choose cannabis tailored to your needs, but you can use your eyes, nose, and common sense to select high-quality flowers.

Once you're at the dispensary, ask to smell the cannabis you're interested in. Top-shelf cannabis will have a pungent aroma that varies depending on the terpenes (the oils that give cannabis its distinct aroma). The buds should be green or purple in color, with orange hairs, and covered in little crystal-like structures called trichomes. These indicate potent cannabis bud. Avoid buying anything brown, dry, or moldy.

Ultimately, the best indicator of the right bud for you is the one you feel drawn to at the dispensary or one that you've reacted to well in the past. We all react to cannabis differently, so if you find something that works for you, trust yourself first and foremost.

Where can I safely obtain high-quality CBD?

CBD is available nationwide in the US, primarily through oils and tinctures. While it's wonderful news that so many people have access to this plant medicine, the CBD market is unregulated, and there are companies out there simply interested in making money. As a result, there is a lot of low-quality CBD on the market that can contain unsafe additives and chemicals. To ensure you're buying high-quality CBD oil, shop online or at your local CBD shop and avoid the stuff at gas stations. Most reputable cannabis brands now sell hemp CBD oil. Just like with cannabis oil, a quick Google search of a product should bring up results from sites such as *Leafly* that review oils.

You can also look at the extraction method. Avoid CBD made with toxic solvents such as butane, hexane, and propane. Ethanol, or grain alcohol, is a safe extraction method although it does remove some of the rich plant waxes that carry added health benefits. CO_2 extraction is also safe. Olive oil can be used as a natural extraction method, although this method is not commonly seen in large-scale production. CBD companies should list on their website and packaging how extraction is done.

CBD can be extracted from marijuana, with low doses of THC, or from the hemp plant, with almost nonexistent THC levels. If you live in a nonlegal state, hemp is what's available. There are claims that CBD works best with a little THC, but due to federal regulation, scientific evidence is minimal, and we're still learning how various cannabinoids interact with one another. That said, what researchers generally agree upon is that, whatever the reason, cannabis, including CBD, works best when as much of the plant is used as possible. This is called the entourage effect, and assumes that CBD is most effective when other cannabinoids, terpenes, and plant chemicals join the party. This is true for hemp-derived CBD as well. Look for the words "whole plant" or "full spectrum" as opposed to "isolate" to enjoy the entourage effect.

Where can I safely obtain cannabis accessories?

After you buy your cannabis or CBD, it's natural to want to stock up on accessories, such as rolling papers, bowls, bongs, vaporizers, ashtrays, grinders, and more. To learn which consumption manner is best for you, see "Various Intake Options and Their Effects" in the section How to Use This Book. Most towns have a local head shop where you can explore pipes and various paraphernalia to find what's right for you. Smoking accessories come in a range of materials, such as glass and wood, and you can even find pipes made of rose quartz on *Etsy*. Reputable online cannabis accessory retailers include *Leafly* and *420 Science*. That being said, you don't have to break the bank to enjoy cannabis. A pack of rolling papers or simple pipe and a lighter work just as well as fancy equipment.

FURTHER READING

Online Connections

Arcane Alchemy

www.arcane-alchemy.com

Green Flower

www.green-flower.com

The National Center for Biotechnology Information

www.ncbi.nlm.nih.gov

Marijuana Doctors

www.marijuanadoctors.com

Medical Marijuana

www.medicalmarijuana.com

Project CBD

www.projectcbd.org

Online Magazines

420 Intel

www.420intel.com

High Times

https://hightimes.com

LA Weekly

www.laweekly.com

Leafly

www.leafly.com

Lifehacker

https://lifehacker.com

MassRoots

www.massroots.com

US/Metric Conversion Chart

VOLUME CONVERSIONS	
US Volume Measure	**Metric Equivalent**
⅛ teaspoon	0.5 milliliter
¼ teaspoon	1 milliliter
½ teaspoon	2 milliliters
1 teaspoon	5 milliliters
½ tablespoon	7 milliliters
1 tablespoon (3 teaspoons)	15 milliliters
2 tablespoons (1 fluid ounce)	30 milliliters
¼ cup (4 tablespoons)	60 milliliters
⅓ cup	90 milliliters
½ cup (4 fluid ounces)	125 milliliters
⅔ cup	160 milliliters
¾ cup (6 fluid ounces)	180 milliliters
1 cup (16 tablespoons)	250 milliliters
1 pint (2 cups)	500 milliliters
1 quart (4 cups)	1 liter (about)

WEIGHT CONVERSIONS	
US Weight Measure	**Metric Equivalent**
½ ounce	15 grams
1 ounce	30 grams
2 ounces	60 grams
3 ounces	85 grams
¼ pound (4 ounces)	115 grams
½ pound (8 ounces)	225 grams
¾ pound (12 ounces)	340 grams
1 pound (16 ounces)	454 grams

OVEN TEMPERATURE CONVERSIONS	
Degrees Fahrenheit	**Degrees Celsius**
200 degrees F	95 degrees C
250 degrees F	120 degrees C
275 degrees F	135 degrees C
300 degrees F	150 degrees C
325 degrees F	160 degrees C
350 degrees F	180 degrees C
375 degrees F	190 degrees C
400 degrees F	205 degrees C
425 degrees F	220 degrees C
450 degrees F	230 degrees C

BAKING PAN SIZES	
American	**Metric**
8 × 1½ inch round baking pan	20 × 4 cm cake tin
9 × 1½ inch round baking pan	23 × 3.5 cm cake tin
11 × 7 × 1½ inch baking pan	28 × 18 × 4 cm baking tin
13 × 9 × 2 inch baking pan	30 × 20 × 5 cm baking tin
2 quart rectangular baking dish	30 × 20 × 3 cm baking tin
15 × 10 × 2 inch baking pan	30 × 25 × 2 cm baking tin (Swiss roll tin)
9 inch pie plate	22 × 4 or 23 × 4 cm pie plate
7 or 8 inch springform pan	18 or 20 cm springform or loose bottom cake tin
9 × 5 × 3 inch loaf pan	23 × 13 × 7 cm or 2 lb narrow loaf or pâté tin
1½ quart casserole	1.5 liter casserole
2 quart casserole	2 liter casserole

Index

About the Author

SOPHIE SAINT THOMAS is a freelance writer based in Brooklyn, originally from the US Virgin Islands. *High Times* named her one of its 2018 "100 Women in High Places" for her writing on cannabis. She has been published in *GQ*, *Playboy*, *Vice*, *Cosmopolitan*, *Forbes*, *Allure*, *Glamour*, *Marie Claire*, *High Times*, *Nylon*, *Refinery29*, *Complex*, *Harper's Bazaar*, *Pride*, *Self*, and more.